LAYLA

DEREK AND THE DOMINOS

AND OTHER ASSORTED LOVE SONGS

Jan Reid

RODALE

for Kip Stratton

Notice
Internet addresses and telephone numbers given in this book were
accurate at the time it went to press.

Rodale books may be purchased for business or promotional use or
for special sales. For information, please write to:
Special Markets Department, Rodale, Inc., 733 Third Avenue,
New York, NY 10017

Printed in the United States of America
Rodale Inc. makes every effort to use acid-free ♾, recycled paper ♲.

Book design by Drew Frantzen

Library of Congress Cataloging-in-Publication Data
Reid, Jan.
    Layla and other assorted love songs by Derek and the Dominos /
Jan Reid.
        p.   cm.
    Includes bibliographical references and discography (p.   ).
    ISBN-13 978-1-59486-369-1   hardcover
    ISBN-10 1-59486-369-5   hardcover
    1. Clapton, Eric.   2. Rock musicians—England—Biography.
3. Derek and the Dominoes (Musical group)   I. Title.
ML419.C58R45   2006
782.42166092'2—dc22   2006024047
[B]

Distributed to the book trade by Holtzbrinck Publishers

2   4   6   8   10   9   7   5   3   1 hardcover

CONTENTS

ACKNOWLEDGMENTS

IN A WAY, this book began in a bar in Dallas in 1969. A boyhood friend and argumentative law student who was predisposed to harrumph loudly about any music composed after the 18th century was telling me that, compared with civilized violinists and oboists and so on, all rock 'n' roll musicians were little better than players of rubber-band ukuleles and combs with tissue paper. I walked over to a jukebox, dropped a quarter or two, and made him listen to a song and my contention that he was full of baloney. The song was "Crossroads" by Cream and their lead guitarist, Eric Clapton.

Clapton and I were born within 12 days of each other in 1945. That's irrelevant, except that it helps explain the clear channel and broad swath his music blew through my youth. Like most Americans who discovered the album, I caught up with *Layla and Other Assorted Love Songs* 2 or 3 years after its release, when FM disc jockeys started playing the sad but thrilling title song, which in turn led to the other amazing songs of an already defunct band, Derek and the Dominos. I played to ruin an LP and multiple cassette recordings of the album while struggling through a succession of love affairs with young women that ended badly before I met the one, Dorothy, who remains my wife today. (*Layla* is one of her favorite records, too.) At some point in the late seventies, a fascinating story began to penetrate my awareness, through the media of pop culture and fan rumor, about the real love affair that inspired Clapton to find his American band and create the song and album.

In late 2004, when my writer friend Kip Stratton told me about Rodale's new Rock of Ages series and put me in touch with its editor, Pete Fornatale, *Layla* was the only album I considered proposing. Kip is the one person who would remember in the course of a boxing gym workout that a novel I wrote 20 years ago had for its epigram a few lines from "Bell Bottom Blues." Pete saw the book in the short letter I wrote, entrusted the project to a writer with just one prior book about music on his résumé, and in the end provided a thorough, knowing edit that revealed a better way of telling the story. My friend and agent David McCormick has been my sounding board and safeguard in the business since the days when he was my best editor at *Texas Monthly*. Larry Bromley and Craig Hillis, authors and musicians whom I've known since the early seventies, dug up essential articles and interviews and helped me understand more about playing the guitar—I'm not a musician. I'm indebted to all these people, and to the characters who made the writing of this book such a rich experience for me.

v

PROLOGUE:
LEGENDS AND LOVE SONGS

And if she winds up walking the streets
Loving every other man she meets
Who'll be the one to answer why?
Lord, I hope it's not me

—Bobby Whitlock,
"Thorn Tree in the Garden"

THE GUITAR PLAYER was barely 20 when the moronic graffiti began to appear in London: "Clapton Is God." What could he do about that but squirm? All he'd done was play. Ambivalent about his fame and fiercely stubborn about the kind of music he cared to play, Eric Clapton had a habit of walking out on gigs without having another lined up. He had been a member of the Yardbirds, John Mayall and the Blues-breakers, Cream, and Blind Faith. He had jammed at length with his blues heroes B. B. King and Muddy Waters, with Bob Dylan and Jimi Hendrix; he had recorded behind Aretha Franklin on *Lady Soul*. Still, Clapton was at that point only a knight in rock 'n' roll's hierarchy—the Beatles were the undisputed lords of the realm.

Clapton first met the Beatles in 1964, when they invited the Yardbirds to perform on a Christmas TV special. He and George Harrison chatted about their respective love of the blues and rockabilly, and for a while after that, they'd see each other occasionally. That year, a London model named Pattie Boyd received a casting call for the Beatles' first movie, *A Hard Day's Night*. The 20-year-old Boyd was long legged, blonde, and blue eyed, her cheeks as perfect as a tear. She had major prospects as a model, her look an inspiration to Twiggy, the iconic model of the late sixties. Cast as a school-girl in attire that embarrassed her, Boyd got to exclaim one word in a scene on a train that the madcap musicians had taken over while fleeing from now-forgotten bad people who were out to get them. "Prisoners?" she cried. That proved to be the extent of her career in movies.

Boyd, who had gone out on the set with two striking sisters in miniskirts, had been living with a boyfriend for 2 years, but she reportedly went there hoping to meet and hit it off with George. She said that when she asked him for an autograph for herself and her sisters, "he signed his name and put two kisses each for them, but under mine he put seven kisses. I thought he must like me a little." They married in early 1966, a few weeks before the band started recording *Revolver*.

Clapton met Boyd shortly after her wedding to Harrison. In 1967, during the famed Summer of Love, which also saw the release of *Sergeant Pepper's Lonely Hearts Club Band*, Clapton saw a great deal of the Beatles; after spending several months hanging out with them, he came to think of Harrison as his best friend.

Clapton was increasingly alienated from the notion of the

English supergroup, yet he kept being a part of one. Though the trio Cream made him rich, he came to feel that he had prostituted himself and thwarted his progress as an artist, and the experience of Blind Faith, except for one pleasant and productive recording session, was a nightmare. Seeking privacy, Clapton bought a century-old, 20-room mansion with gardens and pools and a sprawling estate in the verdant Surrey countryside, near the village where he'd grown up south of London. Its name was Hurtwood Edge, and it was only a short drive from the Harrisons' Surrey estate, Esher.

George and Pattie Harrison were delving deeply into Asian faith and philosophy. For a while, at the same time, Clapton answered the call of Christianity. But it was the late sixties, and he was a rock star. He was living with a girl named Alice Ormsby-Gore, who was the daughter of a former British ambassador to the United States. On the other hand, Clapton admittedly nurtured a boyhood fantasy to sleep with a thousand women before he was done. He took advantage of the abundant opportunities and the permissive sexual mores of the time, as did his married friend George Harrison. Clapton reflected on the prevailing ethos in a *Rolling Stone* interview: "You come out of school, you know, and you get into a group and you've got thousands of chicks out there. I mean you were at school and you were pimply and no one wanted to know you. And then there you are—on stage, with thousands of little girls screaming their heads off. Man, that's power!"

But Eric Clapton's star power had no effect on one woman, and he was reduced to begging for her affection.

Frank Sinatra, who was no fan of the Beatles, said that "Something," George Harrison's evocation of Pattie's sensuality and grace on *Abbey Road,* was one of the loveliest songs he'd ever heard. Sinatra worked it into his repertoire. "Something" was the first of three classic love songs written in tribute to Pattie Boyd that will long outlive her. The other two, "Layla" and "Wonderful Tonight," were written by Eric Clapton. Over the years she has inspired many other Clapton songs. They offer a one-sided account of their relationship, she has justly observed. She was not some hot-assed groupie who caught a man's ride to the celebrity of tabloids and paparazzi. For all the glamour and good times that came her way, she was always in search of a steadiness, a floor that didn't wobble. Pattie Boyd was aware of her power, knew that she could turn the hearts of men who loved her inside out. Still, she was awed, baffled, and frightened by the intensity of feeling she aroused in Clapton. "Maybe it had more to do with them," she would reflect years later in a London newspaper interview. "Perhaps Eric just wanted what George had." The interviewer claimed she offered that cruelty with a shrug.

"I went to Esher several times," Clapton said, "and every time I went, after a nice time with George and Pattie, I remember feeling a dreadful emptiness—because I was certain I was never going to meet a woman quite that beautiful for myself. I knew that. I knew I was in love. I fell in love with her at first sight—and it got heavier and heavier for me." But then something enormous happened that sped the three of them down the slippery slope. The Beatles broke up.

———

In a region of valleys and springs in central Saudi Arabia, an ancient town named Layla sits amid rich green irrigated fields. Near the town of about 80,000 souls is the bed of the once-shimmering and translucent Lake Layla. The lake is now bone-dry—carried away, a local joke goes, in all those watermelons irrigated by the groundwater. The desolate lake bed is a reminder of the proximity of Rub al-Khali, the dreaded Empty Quarter, where only Bedouins and oil and gas well crews brave the heat and windblown sand.

The name of the town and lake take their name from a Bedouin legend that evolved into the classic love story of Arabic and Persian culture—the equivalent of Romeo and Juliet—that goes back more than a thousand years. It dates from an aristocratic period derided by the ascending Muslim culture that followed as *Jahiliyah,* or "ignorance," in Arabia in the second half of the 7th century.

The legend of Qays and Layla (which some scholars contend is based on fact) has been celebrated in countless poems and songs, an Azerbaijani opera, an Urdu-language film, and interpretations as a Sufi allegory. In one Arabic version, a boy born to nobility falls in love with the beautiful girl on first seeing her at a traditional feast; he kills his camel as an offering to the celebration. Unhinged by his passion, he writes gorgeous poems about his love for Layla, a name that means "of the night," and recites his verse on town streets. Qays's name becomes Majnun, which is given to a particular kind of madman. He is possessed by jinn, a class of spirits that in Muslim demonology often take human form. Majnun's madness is mystical and enraptured, harmful mostly to himself. Majnun is desperate to marry Layla; her father is just as determined to keep them apart. Layla shares Qays's ecstasy, but it's forbidden in their culture to speak openly of one's love for another—as that is considered an insult to the girl's name and honor. The youth wanders in the wilderness, going half-clothed and hungry and singing of his ardor and agony to animals.

The story was passed down in oral tradition and anonymous verse until 1188 A.D., when a regional ruler in the Persian Empire commissioned a widely read poet named Nizami Ganjavi to compose a work embracing the legend. It took Nizami, an Azerbaijani, 9 years to finish his epic. His poem, which embraced five narratives and about 8,000 lines, was called *Khamsah,* "The Quintet."

In Nizami's telling, the boy's father tries to arrange the marriage that the lovers desire, but Layla's father believes that the boy's feverish proclamations have disgraced his daughter. Majnun's sin is worse than if he'd held her naked in his arms, for his behavior violates the secrecy and privacy of divine love. A prince tries to comfort the madman and wages war against Layla's clan to break her father's will. Even in bloodshed and defeat, Layla's father refuses to let them have their way. Layla finds that if she phrases her answers to Majnun's poems in mysterious ways and just floats them out like feathers in the wind, somehow they reach him. But the girl's father gives her in marriage to another man, and Majnun's father dies brokenhearted. Layla writes Majnun a letter of sympathy and swears that she denies her husband the pleasures of her bed, that she will always be faithful to her heart's passion. She writes again when Majnun's mother dies, and asks him to visit her. The prince arranges a meeting, but they can come no closer to each other than 10 paces. Later, Layla's husband dies; her status as a widow requires her to remain in her house and see no one for 2 years.

She withers like the blooms and foliage of a winter-stung garden. The torment eventually causes Layla to give up and die. Majnun weeps on her grave, and then he dies. It's a very sad poem.

———

After the 1969 dissolution of the Beatles' artistic and business empire, the Rolling Stones were still the Stones, though they had been disgraced by the mayhem at their free concert at Altamont. Many English artists still roamed high on the pop charts, but the impetus of rock 'n' roll began to move back to America, in search of the next Elvis Presley, Chuck Berry, Buddy Holly. Exciting music started coming out of unexpected places in the South and Southwest. Macon, Georgia. Austin, Texas. Tulsa, Oklahoma. Lubbock, Texas. Jacksonville, Florida. Spartanburg, South Carolina.

Following the rise and fall of Blind Faith, Clapton holed up in his Surrey estate with some American sidemen steeped in Southern rock. When Clapton met them, they had been playing behind a popular white soul revue, Delaney and Bonnie and Friends. The sidemen quit or were fired and cast their lot with Clapton. None of them would become a household name, but together they generated one of the enduring legends of rock 'n' roll.

Carl Radle was a laconic bass player who was balding and wore glasses. He had grown up in Tulsa and had helped make the Oklahoma oil town into an intriguing subcapital of rock 'n' roll, playing in a variety of clubs and bands with players who included Leon Russell and J. J. Cale. Radle was the definitive laid-back southern rocker, and he had extraordinarily strong and fast hands—the kind of bass player who could steal a show.

———

Jim Gordon had established himself as one of the premier drummers in the Los Angeles recording industry. Since his teens, he had brought sharp beats and sheer muscle to recordings by the Everly Brothers, the Monkees, the Byrds, Mason Williams, Judy Collins, Hoyt Axton, Merle Haggard, and Randy Newman, and he had been ushered into the Bramletts' band and Clapton's circle of professional acquaintances by Leon Russell. Gordon was a tall, rangy guy, and he was always drenched in sweat; playing the drums for him was an athletic event. He had enormous talent and an equally huge entourage of demons.

The third musician was a boy-wonder keyboard player, singer, and songwriter named Bobby Whitlock. With dark curls and a baby face, he was the son of an itinerant Baptist preacher in Arkansas who left his family chopping cotton, for it was the only way they could eat. Whitlock came of age under the watch of famed musicians and producers of a Memphis rhythm and blues label, Stax Records. Delaney and Bonnie Bramlett had plucked Whitlock out of a Memphis honky-tonk when he was barely old enough to drive.

Though they had no inkling yet, Clapton and the three Americans were Derek and the Dominos, minus one. In November 1969 and January 1970, they played in sessions for Clapton's debut solo album. Since the Beatles' demise, George Harrison had been brooding and adrift, but he broke out of his funk and in mid-1970 asked Clapton and his friends to help him record *All Things Must Pass*. "We made our bones, really, on that album with George," Clapton said of the band.

They made their bones all right, working as session players on one of the best albums of the decade. And in answering that call, Clapton got a second shot at his best friend's wife.

The marriage of George and Pattie Boyd Harrison was suddenly in trouble. He was distracted by no longer being a Beatle, and in multiple ways she felt shunted aside. She was attracted to the lithe and handsome guitar player who was around much of the time now, and the total focus Clapton lavished on her was alarming, fascinating, and seductive. During the months that Clapton and his American houseguests were recording with George, a flirtation between friends grew into an infatuation, but she resisted letting it grow into an affair, which only turned up the heat and longing.

That May and June, when Clapton wasn't pouring out his love to her, he was in Apple Studios during the recording sessions for *All Things Must Pass* (his guitar work eventually appeared on 10 tracks). The core studio band was Clapton on lead guitar, Radle on bass, Whitlock on organ and piano, and Gordon on drums. On songs that included the title cut, "What Is Life," "Isn't It a Pity," and a number one hit for Harrison, "My Sweet Lord," Clapton and his American friends were working on riffs, chops, and arrangements that flowed directly into their band in the making.

When the sessions with Harrison wrapped, they started touring, working on their material and chemistry in small clubs across England. The band's name, Derek and the Dominos, was an inside joke: They were about to go out for their first show in a London ballroom when Clapton and an old friend worked up the band name as if they were carrying on a skit for a radio program they listened to as children, *The Goon Show*. "It was a make-believe band," he would say, looking back. "It wasn't me, it was another band.

We were all hiding inside it. Derek and the Dominos—the whole thing was . . . assumed. So it couldn't last. I mean, I had to come out and admit that I was being me. I mean, being Derek was a cover for the fact that I was trying to steal someone else's wife."

In many ways, that tour was the most fun the band would have together. The bass player Carl Radle and the drummer Jim Gordon were as gifted as any rhythm players in the business. Bobby Whitlock played keyboards with quirky, offbeat rhythm, and the amazing songs pouring out of the Dominos' collaboration were as much his as Clapton's. Whitlock was partly responsible for Clapton overcoming his nervousness and emerging as a capable singer. "We didn't want any horns," said the soul-groomed Whitlock, "we didn't want no chicks, we wanted a rock 'n' roll band. My vocal concept was that we approached singing like Sam and Dave did: He sings a line, I sing a line, we sing together."

But Clapton was also creating music born of desperation. He went about it as if it wasn't enough just to know and play the blues—to have a chance at winning Pattie; he had to write and sing them, too.

The slow dance in which they'd been engaged warmed into a short intense affair. When Clapton pressed her to run away with him, she broke it off and sent him into a dire emotional tailspin. But Clapton thought enough of his new band and their emerging material that he fantasized that he might win her over with the sheer power of his new music—in which he adapted and refashioned the Bedouin legend of Majnun and Layla. He asked his manager in London to call Tom Dowd, a former nuclear physicist who was emerging as the top engineer and producer in the business. Dowd booked time in Atlantic's Miami studios for Derek and the Dominos, starting in August 1970.

Another of Dowd's clients was a Southern hippie and guitar player who was every bit as talented as Clapton and Jimi Hendrix. Duane Allman was a master of the slide or "bottleneck" style of playing guitar, and in 1968 he had made himself one of the top session players in rock when he challenged America's reigning soul singer, Wilson Pickett, to record the Beatles' "Hey Jude." Though he was not a songwriter or a singer, Duane was the leader and driving force of the Allman Brothers Band—which had struggled far back in the pack behind the likes of the Beatles and Cream but was now on a fast track to stardom.

Allman's addition as the fifth Domino was as much a fluke as the band's name. Dowd had helped oversee the move of Atlantic's Southern base of operations to Criteria Recording Studios in Miami. When Derek and the Dominos arrived and started recording, the Allman Brothers happened to have a concert booked in Miami, and Dowd took Clapton to the concert; they sat on the floor right under the stage. As Allman started playing a solo, he recognized Clapton and for a few beats was awestruck.

After the concert, Allman and the rest of the band went back to the studios, and they jammed with Derek and the Dominos all night. Unlike the rest of the Allman Brothers Band, Duane hung around and kept playing. Though one can say he was only a session player—his schedule allowed him to appear with the band in just a handful of concert dates—his bottleneck play was all over the record, complementing and elevating Clapton's style. Allman became a band leader in a way, always riffing and improvising, and it was his suggestion that gave Clapton the signature lines of the defining song of his career. For all the pain of its themes there was an uplifting sweetness in the melodies and harmonies the guitarists composed. It was also dance music—sexy as all get-out.

Clapton would never be a Bob Dylan or Leonard Cohen or Bruce Springsteen. As poetry, his lyrics have always lain somewhat flat on the page. But he understood that the magic of songwriting lies in deceptive simplicity, and his genius is his ability to find enormous breadth and range within the few notes and basic chords of an electric lead guitar. During the sessions Clapton heard the drummer Jim Gordon on a piano plunking a tune that he hoped to put on an album of his own someday. Clapton prevailed on Gordon to let them have it. Splicing in the coda was a delicate task for Dowd, and it carried the song over 7 minutes, a risky venture that might result in the song not receiving airplay because of length. But after all these years, you hear Clapton's voice breaking with raw sorrow and the piercing then soaring notes of those guitars on "Layla" and you know what's coming next. And you know what to do—you turn it up.

The real-life story of Clapton's love of the woman who inspired "Layla" was far from over in 1970. Neither was his friendship with George Harrison. As those three continued to punish each other, the record that seemed and sounded so right in the Miami studio was at first a commercial flop. It never made the charts in England, and 2 years passed before "Layla" caught fire on FM stations in the United States. By then Clapton was on a self-destructive bender of heroin addiction. With Allman busy in his own band, Derek and the rest of the Dominos had played one 50-date tour that climaxed with a concert at the Fillmore East in New York. That recording at the Fillmore would be Derek and the Dominos' only follow-up to *Layla and Other Assorted Love Songs*.

After they awarded themselves that name, the band lasted just 11 months. Whitlock got them to play in sessions for his well-deserved solo album at studios outside London. But 4 months later, in May 1971, the band broke up in those studios in the middle of an ego-ridden and drug-jangled session that laid down 13 tracks but was going nowhere. Clapton and Gordon got in a heated argument, doors slammed, and the band never got together again. Clapton would say, "I remember to this day being in my home, feeling totally lost and hearing Bobby Whitlock pull up in the driveway outside and scream to me to come out. He sat in his car outside all day, and I hid. And that's when I went into my journey into smack."

At its best, rock 'n' roll is a celebration of electric guitars, and those 1970 studio sessions brought together two musicians who could have been virtuosos if they had lived and played in the time of Mozart. But the collaboration of Clapton and Allman provided just one level of the record's beauty. Clapton and Whitlock's songs exceeded their abilities as singers, and captured a time in their lives when they were mature enough to know what soaring heights erotic love could bring, and what a craven mess they could and probably would make of it.

To hear those guitars and voices is to remember precisely what the world was like when you were 25, when you couldn't seem to get any love right, and that was the only thing that mattered.

1

BLUESMAN

ERIC PATRICK CLAPTON was born March 30, 1945, in a two-story brick residence in the village of Ripley, 30 miles south of London. The Allies' triumph was just months away, but the tumult and dislocation of the war left him with about as strange a childhood as any boy could bear. His mother, Pat Clapton, took her last name from her father, who died when she was a child; she raised in Ripley by her mother, Rose, and her stepfather, a plasterer and bricklayer named Jack Clapp. Pat Clapton had a brief romance with a Canadian airman named Edward Fryer who was stationed nearby and played piano in swing dance bands; they met at one of his gigs, and she got pregnant. But Fryer had a wife in Canada, and he went home to her as soon as the war was over. Pat Clapton was 16 when Eric was born.

Surrey County is today one of the most affluent locales in Europe, part of the lush Green Belt known for horse farms, cricket matches, and biking trails. But the hamlet of Clapton's birth was a straitlaced working-class town surrounded by farmland—a time and a place that was hard on teenage single mothers and their children. Condemnation of the girl in the village was cruel. There were angry rows within the house as well. When her son was 2, Pat Clapton left him with her mother and stepfather. She followed another Canadian serviceman to his next posting in Germany; they subsequently married and moved to Canada. But the pretense carried out by the family in Ripley was mind boggling: Eric Clapton began life believing that his grandparents were his parents and that his uncle Adrian, who had moved back home after his tour in the service, was his cool older brother.

Eric's grandmother claimed that they told Eric the truth as soon as he started school at age 5. Perhaps they did, but in his recollection, he was 9 when he absorbed this bewildering news. He never met his father, and when his mother reappeared, it was with Eric's younger half-brother and a Canadian husband who had uncertain knowledge of her past. So a decision was made within the family to persist with the fiction, even when the parties were under the same roof. An elaborate ruse that was meant to protect Eric backfired in his social confidence and schoolwork: "I was doing really well," he told one writer. "Then my real mum came back to stay with us. From that moment they say I was moody and nasty and wouldn't try. We had to go through this whole thing of pretending she was my sister."

Nevertheless, Clapton claimed he "had a lovely time growing up." His grandparents, whom he called Mum and Dad, were "very fun-loving people." Rose Clapp used to play a piano and get them all singing at night, and they encouraged Rick, as they called him then, to act out performances when they had guests. On Saturday mornings, Eric would listen to *The Goon Show,* a popular program for children—amid the banter and fifties novelty records, the show would sometimes air "Hound Dog" by Elvis Presley and "Ain't That a Shame" by Fats Domino. "The first blues song I ever heard was on that program," Clapton would reminisce. "It was a song by Sonny Terry and Brownie McGhee, with Sonny Terry howling and playing the harmonica. It blew me away."

Television and its embrace of the new American phenomenon, rock 'n' roll, swept him up in 1958. "It was like seeing someone from outer space," Clapton said of watching Jerry Lee Lewis perform "Great Balls of Fire." "And I realized suddenly that here I was in this village that was never going to change, yet there on TV was something out of the future. And I wanted to go there!" Clapton was riveted by the leaping wild man and the bass guitar in the small backup band. At that point, he didn't know the difference between a lead guitar and a bass guitar. He just knew that he wanted one.

He tried to carve one out of a block of wood, and he ragged his family until they bought him a plastic guitar merchandised under the name of Elvis Presley. On Clapton's 13th birthday, his grandparents bought him a real acoustic guitar, a Spanish model. Without instruction, he tried to learn to play by ear. He chanced upon the A and D chords and believed he had invented them. He would sit at the top of the stairs at home and create an echo akin to what he heard on records.

Despite the solace he took in his new hobby, Clapton was confused and tormented by the revelations about his family—and who and what all this made of him. He became an introverted loner with a chip on his shoulder. "I wanted to be a beatnik before beatniks were even heard of in Ripley," he said. "I was the village beatnik." Clapton offered memories of having rocks thrown at him by bullies because he was a skinny "seven stone [98-pound] weakling." He hung out with a small clique of schoolyard misfits that others called "the loonies." After he became a rock star, his grandmother told one interviewer, "I can sit and cry when he plays the blues. He was always a lonely boy, and his music still gives me that feel about him. We all loved him so much, there was no need for him to be lonely."

Before the downspin of his performance at school, he had impressed his teachers with his aptitude for art. His grandparents encouraged him to pursue a career as a commercial artist, and they got him into a school with a curriculum that allowed him to focus on his area of interest and talent. He applied himself and did well on his final exams; that record of achievement and his portfolio won him conditional admission to the Kingston-on-Thames College of Art in 1961. But he regretted his decision to pursue the graphics art route, with a specialty in stained glass design. He wished he could make friends among the Bohemian types who were on the fine arts side. Trying to impress them, Clapton pulled stunts like showing up drunk at lunch, and before long his grandparents received a letter from the Kingston headmaster warning that Eric was in danger of blowing his probation if he did not finish his work and stop cutting class. Clapton was in fact applying himself and becoming a formidable scholar. It just wasn't at school.

In his room he spent countless hours trying to unlock a guitar's secrets. His grandmother remarked that the nightly discordant noise could be maddening. But, as always, the family indulged him by buying him a portable reel-to-reel recorder, and he fancied that the results sounded like the records of

Elvis Presley, Chuck Berry, and Buddy Holly. But that was not the style that bewitched him. The alienated small-town English youth followed rock 'n' roll back to its origins, which to his ear was purer stuff: the blues.

One of the most important early influences on him was Big Bill Broonzy. Born in Mississippi in the 1890s, Broonzy fled rural poverty and racism and moved to Chicago in 1924. He often scuffled for a living as a janitor and sometime preacher but became one of the city's leading bluesmen in the thirties and forties. Broonzy played acoustic guitar backed by musicians on a small set of drums and a stand-up bass, often with a harmonica or horns. He preceded and strongly influenced the electrified Chicago blues that emerged in the late forties and fifties on the shoulders of T-Bone Walker, Muddy Waters, and Howlin' Wolf. The ascendance of the electrified bluesmen moved Broonzy aside with black audiences and on the charts of "race records." Rather than change his style of playing, Broonzy shared bills with white folksingers such as Pete Seeger. He carried on until his death from throat cancer in 1958, and he played a major role in popularizing American blues in Europe, leaving songs that would thrive in rock tributes long after his name was mostly forgotten—among them "C. C. Rider" and "Key to the Highway."

Clapton's amateur musicology also led him to Tampa Red Whittaker. With fair skin and red hair, the "Guitar Wizard" migrated from Florida to Chicago and for a while worked the street corners, gaining renown with a bawdy, ragtime-derived hit called "It's Tight Like That" in 1928. He performed in a faddish Depression-era group called the Hokum Boys, and after the repeal of Prohibition, his home became a booking agency, rehearsal space, and salon for local blues players. Tampa Red's gifts included a slide guitar style in which he ignored chords with his right hand and relied on quick-fingered single-string runs. Tampa Red was a boozer, and after his wife died in 1953, his remaining years in Chicago were not kind to him. He passed away destitute in 1981.

Another hero of Clapton was Blind Willie Johnson. Born about 1902, Johnson came from small towns in the cotton-farming country between Dallas and Houston. Willie Johnson's mother died when he was small, and when his father caught his next wife sleeping with another man, he beat her. She took revenge by throwing lye in his 7-year-old son's face, blinding him. The father used to put Blind Willie out on the street of a town called Hearne every Saturday with a tin cup tied around his neck. Blind Willie made his way with blues songs fashioned from gospel, but he was best known for strumming bass figures with his thumb while composing melodies by sliding a penknife along the higher strings. Johnson passed away before the age of 50. His house burned down, and he caught pneumonia from sleeping on a cold, wet pallet.

But the lackadaisical English art student and would-be beatnik responded to the artistry and legend of Robert Johnson more than any other blues singer and guitar player. Born in Hazlehurst, Mississippi, in about 1910, Johnson spent a great deal of his short life trying to transcend the Delta country. Johnson's guitar playing relied on rolling rhythms drawn mostly from bass strings, but he also studied the bottleneck technique of Tampa Red and in his singing adapted the "blue yodel" of the white country singer Jimmie Rodgers, known as the "Singing Brakeman."

Johnson played with young Howlin' Wolf and was a mentor of Muddy Waters. Johnson was a hit-chasing pop singer, but some of his best guitar pieces had phrasings of jazz. One admirer described Johnson's playing as "sharp fingers fluttering like a trapped bird." He often performed with his back turned to the audience. Some interpreted that as a facet of his churlish temperament—to others, the habit signified that he didn't want to give away any of his tricks.

These days Johnson is hyped as "King of the Delta Blues," but in fact he was more the blues equivalent of James Dean. He had just two studio sessions; his recorded body of work from those sessions amounts to 29 songs. A record producer set him up at San Antonio's Gunter Hotel in November 1936. As the story has it, he went for a stroll and got arrested for vagrancy; he then smart-mouthed the white cops, who cracked his head and smashed his guitar. If that's true, he possessed or acquired a good spare, for during that session he recorded "Come On in My Kitchen." In the song's story, a man who had run off with the lover of his best friend experienced the misery of seeing the friend steal her back. For guitarists, the sublime achievement of the piece came in a ghostly, keening, onomatopoeic slide progression, with Johnson's whispered bridge about a howling wind.

The central act of Johnson's "Crossroads Blues" was flagging a ride—hitchhiking. But Son House advanced the hokum that one night at the juncture of the Delta's Highway 61 and Highway 49, Johnson had sold his soul to the devil in exchange for his supernatural ability to play the guitar. Johnson didn't live to see 30. There's conjecture that he was stabbed to death, or died of syphilis, or was poisoned with strychnine by a man who didn't take kindly to being cuckolded by the bluesman. It's likely that his death in August 1938 was caused by pneumonia, but the Delta bluesman Sonny Boy Williamson added to the myth: "I heard that it was something to do with the Black Arts. Before he died, Robert was crawling along the ground on all fours: barking and snapping like a mad beast. That was what the poison done to him."

Johnson was a brilliant guitarist who made his reputation with lyrics about men who lived by the gun and knife and considered women property that could be rightly owned and stolen. In fact, he appeared to despise women, apart from feel-good sojourns between their thighs. The teenage Clapton did not invent the glamorization of the superstitions and domestic violence of poor black Americans, any more than he invented the 12-note blues progression. But the blues was his rhapsody, and Robert Johnson was his hero. "Up until I heard his music," Clapton would write on the notes of a tribute record, "everything I had ever heard seemed as if it was dressed up for a shop window somewhere, so that when I heard him for the first time, it was like he was singing only for himself, and now and then, maybe God."

Clapton would fold Johnson's "Crossroads Blues" and "Traveling Riverside Blues" into his "Crossroads," a faithful, randy tribute to Johnson and the chosen signature of Clapton's rock 'n' roll career. Long before Clapton heard about the legend of Layla and obsessed with desire for his best friend's wife, he was putting the bulge in his blue jeans front and center in his music.

———

Clapton was stunned when the headmaster of the Kingston art college looked at his thin portfolio and made good on his promise to expel him, after just a year. Clapton took a turn mixing cement and mortar for his grandfather at his construction sites. It didn't take him long to tire of manual labor; out of work, he found himself sleeping on friends' floors and on park benches. "I didn't know what to do," he said, "so I asked my family to get me an electric guitar. It became clear that I would have to make a go of it." As always, the Clapps came through for him, paying £100 in installments for a red American Kay model. He started playing in folk clubs in Surrey towns and in the West End, first in a guitar duo and then in a five-piece band, nattily clad in coats and narrow ties, called the Roosters.

Clapton was awed by the Beatles' outpouring of songs and the commercial sensation they were causing. Still, ever the bluesman, he listened to T-Bone Walker and B. B. King and said a defining moment for him came on hearing the bent notes of the electric guitar lead on "I Love the Woman" by a veteran blues singer and guitarist from Texas and then Chicago, Freddie King. Clapton and the Roosters were just one of the groups dedicated to American rhythm and blues in England in early 1963. Eric Burdon and the Animals were the hottest band in Newcastle, while the Spencer Davis Group and their 16-year-old singer Stevie Winwood were celebrities in Birmingham. In London, Clapton mingled with blues aficionados at a teen hangout called the Ealey Blues Club and on Thursday R&B Night at the Marquee. At the Crawdaddy Club in Richmond, Clapton saw a great deal of the house band, a lively and posturing bunch who named themselves the Rolling Stones in tribute to the Muddy Waters song.

Clapton first made an impression on the Yardbirds with cocksure and vocal critiques of their gigs around Kingston. He told them that he was a better lead guitarist than anyone they had tried, and in October 1963 they hired him. The Stones' debut single had meanwhile got them an English tour with the Everly Brothers and Bo Diddley, and the Yardbirds inherited their gig as the house band at the Crawdaddy. Soon after Clapton joined the band, Sonny Boy Williamson decided to stay in England after appearing at the American Blues Festival in Croydon. He picked up the Yardbirds for his backup group. Here was a man with direct lineage to Robert Johnson, but Clapton found the old bluesman a hard taskmaster. "When Sonny Boy came over we didn't know how to back him up," Clapton said. "It was frightening, really, because this man was real and we weren't. He wasn't very tolerant, either. He did take a shine to us after a while, but before that he put us through some bloody hard paces."

Clapton had a happier time months later when he was brought in by pianist Otis Spann for a recording session where he met and played with Spann's half-brother, Muddy Waters. "Initially I was very shy with Muddy," Clapton said. "I was in awe. He was like the father of it all. And so whenever I was around him, I tried to be as humble as possible and not start conversations, just let it come from him. As a result, I never pushed him in a researcher's way; I never asked him questions that I thought would be irritating. Like, I didn't want to ask him if he knew Robert Johnson."

Rejecting the mod look popularized by other English rockers, Clapton's style then was avant garde Ivy League— short hair, tab-collared shirt, blue jeans rolled in pressed cuffs up to his ankles, a long colorful scarf hung around his neck and shoulders. After Columbia signed the band and recorded *Five Live Yardbirds*, the Yardbirds played a package tour with Jerry Lee Lewis, and the Beatles invited them to the 1964 Christmas TV special where Clapton first struck up a chat with George Harrison.

Despite the band's successes, Clapton came into conflict with the bass player, Paul Samwell-Smith. Clapton thought the bassist was a middle-class brat, a conformist. Samwell-Smith was trendy enough, though, that he knew shaggy locks were in, and he complained when Clapton came back from a trip to visit his mother in Germany with a buzz cut. The guitarist shrugged that his stepfather, who was in the service, wouldn't let him eat on base unless he cut his hair. The Yardbirds' manager appointed Samwell-Smith the leader of the band, and they all overruled Clapton's choice of a second single, an Otis Redding song called "Your One and Only Man." Instead, the single, which shot to number two in England and number six in the States, was "For Your Love."

Clapton was aghast because the instrumental tracks were dominated by session players on harpsichord and bongos. "Where does that leave me?" he asked. "Twelve-string guitar, I suppose." The other Yardbirds thought he was crazy. Didn't he want a hit song? When he told them he was quitting, they were glad to show the malcontent the door. They had already decided to hire Jeff Beck.

At 20, Clapton thought he might be through with playing music for a living. But only 2 weeks after leaving the Yardbirds, he accepted a job with John Mayall and the Bluesbreakers. Mayall was older than the others, and he ran a tight ship. "I used to live at John's house for a long time in a room that was like a cupboard," Clapton said. "He was amazing, man. I mean, no one was allowed to drink!" When Clapton got tired of the music, he impulsively quit another successful band. He and some pals were having a better time drinking wine and listening to blues and jazz. They formed a group called the Glands and declared that they were going to play their way around the world. They got as far as Greece. "We met this club proprietor who hired us to open for a Greek band that played Beatles songs," he said. "Then the Greek band was involved in a terrible road accident in which half of them were killed, and I found myself obliged to play with both bands. I was a quick learner then; I learned all the Beatles and Kinks songs they were doing, and I began to realize that I was trapped, that the proprietor wouldn't let me go. He fired the rest of our band, and I was stuck there, with this Greek band."

The club owner called the police to examine Clapton's friends' visas and shoo them out of the country. Clapton's rock 'n' roll farce ended with him locked up with his gear in an upstairs room at the club. He talked the club owner into letting him go out to get his guitar restrung, which allowed him to escape with his Gibson Les Paul, but he had to sacrifice his clothes and his amp.

When Clapton limped back to England from Greece in November 1965, Mayall gave him his job back. The result was the period when the graffiti began to appear on subway walls and toilet stalls in London: "Clapton Is God." In recognition of his importance, Decca titled John Mayall's 1966 record *Blues Breakers with Eric Clapton*. The Blues Breakers' album reached number six on the English charts that July, but by then the brash 21-year-old had jumped ship again. Jack Bruce had come aboard as the band's bass player for a while, and Clapton was inspired by his ability to change and compose music in the course of playing a piece. When Clapton persuaded the redoubtable drummer Ginger Baker to patch up some old rifts with Bruce and form a group, he gave Mayall just 2 weeks' notice. They named the new band Cream.

2

SUPERSTAR

IN A SPECIAL ISSUE that *Guitar Player* magazine devoted to Eric Clapton's career, the American jazz virtuoso John Etheridge reflected: "All that 'Clapton Is God' business was really genuine. Because he was just like a thunderbolt out of the sky. It must have been like when people first heard Django Reinhardt. I'm not talking about technique or anything, but just hearing something totally new. By the time Clapton got to America, Hendrix had happened. But in England, this was before Hendrix. The first time I saw him, I couldn't believe it—all that vibrato, and the sustain. After that it was like, who could be the first on your block to get a vibrato like Eric's?"

Cream was such a titan of sixties rock that it's hard to remember the volatile and fractious group lasted only 2½ years. Clapton grumbled publicly that the production quality of *Fresh Cream*—which reached number six in England, had a 92-week run on U.S. charts, and launched the band as a worldwide phenomenon—"could have been better." He felt from the start that his devotion to the blues and ambition to sing were always being trumped and thwarted by Ginger Baker and Jack Bruce. Nevertheless, he was often more secure than his strong-willed bandmates. In early 1967 Cream was playing a concert at a school called Central London Polytechnic when their friend Chas Chandler, the bass player of the Animals, brought Jimi Hendrix backstage and asked them if the American sensation could sit in for a couple of songs. Baker's response was especially unenthusiastic and grudging; he feared repercussions in the press if the American showed up their guitar god on Cream's home turf. But Clapton was game to play with anybody.

Clapton's look was changing with the times. Discarding the arch straightness of his earlier look, he grew muttonchop sideburns and let his hair reach his collar. He customarily performed in loafers, jeans, a shirt, and a fur-collared Royal Air Force leather jacket. Hendrix arrived in his fringed coat and necklace and wildly colored silk; Clapton watched him primp before the mirror and tease his Afro to its haloed max. The guitarists said little more than hello, but Clapton was himself awed by the two numbers they played together that night. A rare left-hander, Hendrix played his guitar behind his back, plucked it with his teeth, humped it as if screwing it, and most impressive to Clapton, on an interpretation of Howlin' Wolf's "Killing Floor," he somehow managed to play rhythm and lead at the same time.

Clapton later reflected on that first encounter with Hendrix: "He did everything that he did for the rest of his career in those two songs. It just blew the audience away; they'd never seen anything like it." Weeks later he chanced upon Hendrix again as the Seattle guitarist was being interviewed at a London restaurant. By the end of the evening Hendrix was so taken with his peer and rival that he clutched Clapton's hand, gave him a kiss, and said: "I just kissed the fairest soul brother in England." They were boundless fans of each other and recognized that they were joined together in their skill and stature, but perhaps because opportunity for interaction was limited, they did not become close friends.

But that jam session was an important encounter. Hendrix brought back from playing with Cream a clear recognition of what a star guitarist could do within the structure of a trio; he went back to the States and within weeks formed his own threesome, the Jimi Hendrix Experience. In a superficial way, Hendrix's influence on Clapton could be seen in his adaptation of jewelry, brightly colored silk shirts, skintight pants, and the silliest affectation of his career, a permed faux Afro. On the more important plane of music, Clapton told *Rolling Stone* that he learned from Hendrix that a repertoire of distinction did not have to be entirely limited to the blues.

Clapton was then living in a Pheasantry, Chelsea, loft with a model named Charlotte Martin. The young lovers couldn't have had much privacy, for the rather small flat was also occupied by the poet Pete Brown, the illustrator Martin Sharp, the budding feminist author Germaine Greer, and the cartoonist and journalist-critic Anthony Haden-Guest. Short said, "There were a lot of Australian hangers-on, whose presence Eric usually tolerated. Once a week, he'd throw everyone out and start yelling at Charlotte, berating her for not looking after the place."

Cream's manager, Robert Stigwood, was a flamboyant Australian with a background in theater promotion, but he made himself a music industry juggernaut by following his hunch that Cream would be superstars. Clapton seemed to have no sense of the adult world economy; when he needed money Stigwood gave it to him, like a kid. Food, drink, and merchandise were delivered free to his Chelsea door. Worshipped by England's graffiti scrawlers and a fawning rock 'n' roll press, Clapton was well traveled in Europe but maintained that he was indifferent about seeing America, though he would like to visit the blues shrine of Chicago. Stigwood knew, however, that Cream needed to be big on both sides of the Atlantic. The lead guitarist was suddenly hot to go when Stigwood landed them a 10-day gig on the show of Murray Kaufman in New York's RKO Theater. Kaufman was a radio host, but he put on a stage show that was a throwback to vaudeville. Cream found themselves sharing bills with jugglers and midgets. From stage wings he bellowed "Move! Move!" at the languid Clapton, who in performance was no Chuck Berry or Jerry Lee Lewis.

Though that gig was demeaning, Clapton loved New York. He had a great time at a "be-in" at Central Park, with marijuana and amyl nitrates for the asking. He hung out in the Village with Frank Zappa and jammed at the Café Au Go Go with B. B. King, Elvin Bishop, and Al Kooper. He also took advantage of eager and available flesh. Of growing concern to his management, in interviews Clapton had a gift for immature, boorish, and impolitic remarks.

On the phenomenon of rock groupies: "There are some chicks around who really are fucked up in their heads and as a result they probably were carrying on like that at the time, but afterwards they feel so ashamed that they can't lead a straight life with anyone. They probably think they're whores. But as a rule they're the most incredibly warm people. I mean, there are a few exceptions—chicks who are just out to be superstar groupies because it's the thing to do, but in the early days they were just chicks who wanted to look after you when you were in town. If making love to you was going to make you happy, they'd make love. If you were tired and didn't want to make it, they'd cook you a meal and make you feel at home. They really were 'ports of call.'"

Weeks after his first romp in New York, a return trip brought him into the orbit of Tom Dowd, the most respected engineer in the business. Dowd's studio résumé ranged from John Coltrane to Ray Charles, from Bobby Darin's "Mack the Knife" to Aretha Franklin's "Respect." At the storied Atlantic studios, Dowd was assigned to *Disraeli Gears,* which had to be produced quickly because the musicians only had 3-day visas. Dowd was thunderstruck when Cream's roadies dollied in the huge stacks of amplifiers that the band used in concerts into Atlantic's small studio: "They recorded at an ear-shattering level. I'd never worked with the order of power in the studio that these chaps had."

In an interview with *Guitar Player*, Clapton rejected criticism that in developing the sound of Cream he had forsaken his roots: "Most people say that I'm not playing blues guitar anymore, and I beg to differ, because it's the only thing I can play, you know. I can't play anything else, so everything I do play is blues structurally. I mean, if you say to me, 'Play some Baroque music, play some Indian music, or play anything else except blues,' I wouldn't be able to. . . . See, what the whole thing about the sound is, is just the old blues sound, but heavily amplified—a lot louder."

Stigwood raised eyebrows by passing on the Monterey

pop festival, but Cream kicked off their first U.S. tour with prestigious bookings—2 weeks at the Fillmore and Winterland in San Francisco, the most fashionable and talked-about city in the rock orbit. The imperial Stigwood strode into the Fillmore and asked to be shown to his table beside the stage; the crusty impresario Bill Graham took pleasure in telling the dandy to find a seat on the floor. That American tour was both Cream's zenith and a foreshadowing of the band's demise.

The sheer volume that Clapton had bragged about was taking a drastic toll on him and his ability. "When we were playing at the Fillmore for a while, I was wearing specially designed ear plugs. I had to, because I couldn't hear anything anymore. I was playing full volume in a kind of weird, traumatic state, knowing that I had to play and not really wanting to. I was deaf, and I couldn't hear anything. And I was wearing these earplugs, and I couldn't hear through them. And I was really just brought down."

In a San Francisco hotel, Baker and Bruce got in a brawl involving a fire extinguisher. After that, when the trio arrived in another city, they stayed with different friends or in separate hotels, avoiding each other until it was concert time. "There was a constant battle between Ginger and Jack," Clapton relates. "They loved one another's playing but couldn't stand the sight of each other. I was the mediator and getting tired of that."

During those weeks, Clapton spent a few days getting to know the Band in Woodstock, New York, at Robbie Robertson's invitation. Clapton liked them immensely, and someone passed him a bootleg copy of Dylan and the Band in *The Basement Tapes*, which circulated at the same time as the group's influential first album, *Music from Big Pink*. Clapton described his reassessment of his music and himself: "I got hold of an acetate of the Band, listened to it and thought, 'What's going on?' I'm in a group that's a raging success, it's a *con*, it makes a lot of money, I'm trying to appreciate it, and here's a band that's been working for 10 years and *that's* where I'd like to be."

It's hard now to listen to the Band's erratic first efforts and fathom why *Big Pink* was so influential. But something strange had happened to rock music and its darling instrument, the electric lead guitar. Pete Townshend ceased being a nameless sideman of a good British band and became the most notable presence of the Who when he started smashing his piece into plastic shards and coils of quivering wire after every gig. Hendrix upped the ante by dousing his guitars with lighter fluid and setting them on fire. In contrast, Robertson, a guitarist and arranger whom Clapton respected immensely, articulated the clear-eyed contrariness of these guys holed up in a cold house in upstate New York: "We were rebelling against the rebellion. Whatever was happening. If everybody was going west, then we were going east and never once discussed it. . . . It was an instinct to separate ourselves from the pack."

Clapton was spun on his heel by the Band's melodic arrangements, their vivid storytelling, and Robertson's insistence on doing away with those long, screaming guitar solos— which in his case he likened to premature ejaculations—and making the compositions charge forth with short explosive riffs. "Well, this is what I wanted to play," Clapton remembered thinking, "not extended solos and maestro bullshit, just good funky songs."

Yet Clapton brimmed with contradictions. He was a different man when he got back to England from that U.S. tour. Despite his weariness with Cream's constant ego strife and his thinly veiled contempt for what the band was playing, he did not veer toward the stripped-down style of the Band. To the contrary, he seemed to embrace for the first time the idea of being a pop star. He began to use the wah-wah pedal and mimicked the feedback squawks of Hendrix. Onstage now he frolicked and boogied. In the glow of their extravagant success, Clapton came out to play a show at the Saville Theatre in London wearing a kimono, beads, necklace, and makeup. Clapton made up his mind to remove all doubt about who was the real star of this show, who was the real boss of this show. At the climax of the Saville Theatre concert, he suspended his guitar from the ceiling by a chain to maximize the feedback. Then he lay down onstage and closed his eyes for a while. The poor young man needed rest.

The Saville Theatre show was a celebrity event, with an elite party afterward. In the crowd and at the party that night were George and Pattie Harrison. In the 2 years of her marriage to George, Pattie had occasionally been around Eric, but there were a lot of young musicians with eyes for her. At the party after the Saville Theatre performance, she studied his martyr's air, and for the first time, she was intrigued. Clapton "didn't talk to anybody or socialize," the beauty would recall. "There was an aura about him that set him apart from the others. Definitely."

Born in 1943, George Harrison had grown up the son of a Liverpool bus driver. The kid wore blue suede shoes before anyone there had heard of Carl Perkins or Elvis Presley, and he wrecked his studies by devoting all his focus on playing guitar. Harrison and Clapton had so much in common that it was almost inevitable they became close friends. At the Apple Studios at year's end in 1967, Clapton played in sessions for Harrison on an eclectic soundtrack for a movie called *Wonderwall*; their guitars were juxtaposed with sitar, sarod, tabla, and tambura played by Indian musicians. The next year often found Clapton staying at Esher, the Harrisons' retreat in Surrey. Sometimes Charlotte Martin came with Eric, but usually it was just the Harrisons and him.

Clapton had first dropped LSD in Scotland on a cover shoot for *Disraeli Gears*. His fairly brief experience with acid ended with a very bad trip. "I just thought I was going to die. But, I mean, it was all right because I thought, well, if I'm going to die it doesn't matter. I'll just go and lie somewhere. So I went into a room, lay down on a bed, and waited to die. I can remember people coming in and saying, 'Are you all right?' and me saying, 'Oh yes. Leave me alone. I'm dying.'"

Rebuked by a Scandinavian critic for behaving like "Mick Jagger with a guitar," Clapton answered by playing a whole show with his back to the audience, à la Robert Johnson. The massive hype surrounding Cream inevitably boomeranged on its lead guitarist: In May 1968, *Rolling Stone* ran a blistering review of a Cream concert. Calling Clapton "a master of the blues clichés of all the post–World War II blues guitarists," the critic Jon Landau went on to say that "Clapton's problem is that while he has vast potential, at this time he hasn't begun to fulfill it. He is a virtuoso at performing other people's ideas." Clapton was infuriated and devastated, but the salvo echoed his own disdain for what the band had become and what he believed was his lack of growth as an artist: "The [*Rolling Stone*] piece and *Big Pink* convinced me I was going to pull out of Cream."

When Clapton wasn't off playing, he was increasingly scarce around the flat at Pheasantry. When he wasn't with George and Pattie, he had a circuit of in-crowd nightclubs where he drank, talked, and checked out new bands, and he started hanging out in the Chelsea home of Keith Richards. He sat in with the Stones on *Let It Bleed*'s "Love in Vain" and was widely rumored to be in line to succeed guitarist Brian Jones, who was in trouble with the band. But Clapton always had a strong bond with his home village, Ripley. The native son and past teen misfit would show up in Afghan attire to buy a pack of cigarettes and chat up the working folk.

In Harrison's car, George and Eric roamed the Surrey countryside looking for a new home that would be close to London, Ripley, and Esher. Clapton made an excellent real estate investment in Hurtwood Edge, a 20-room Italianate mansion just a few kilometers from where he grew up. Back in Chelsea, Charlotte Martin received a farewell note from Clapton expressing hope that they would always be friends. He was involved with another model, Cathy James, as well as with Pattie's younger sister, Paula Boyd. Then, ensconced at Hurtwood Edge, he embarked on a long relationship with Alice Ormsby-Gore, the daughter of Lord David Harlech, a former British ambassador to the United States. She was barely 17 when she came around one day with a group of interior decorators.

But Clapton was always coming back to Esher to play and talk with George and inwardly obsess over his pain and love for his best friend's wife. Though George was a well-known philanderer, Pattie loved him; she tolerated his infidelities and increasingly distant mysticism, trying to make their marriage work. For Pattie, the flirtation with Eric was warming into desire, but she was determined to keep their relationship platonic. Clapton observed the pretense that he only wanted to be her good friend. He later admitted that he was closing his eyes and imagining Pattie during times when he was in her sister Paula's arms.

In late summer of 1968, Cream's "Sunshine of Your Love" shot up the charts in both England and the States. Meanwhile the Beatles started recording their eponymous record known as the *White Album*. Harrison's composition of "While My Guitar Gently Weeps" had been partly inspired by his reading the *I Ching*. He recorded a fine acoustic demo, but he was dissatisfied with his attempts to capture the lead solo. Harrison said, "I worked on that song with John, Paul, and Ringo one day, and they were not interested at all. And I knew inside of me that it was a nice song. The next day I was with Eric, and I was going into the session, and I said, 'We're going to do this song. Come on and play on it.' He said, 'Oh, no. I can't do that. Nobody ever plays on Beatles records.' I said, 'Look, it's my song, and I want you to play on it.' So Eric came in, and the other guys were as good as gold because he was there. Also, it left me free to do the vocal and play rhythm. Then we listened to it back, and he said, 'Ah, there's a problem, though; it's not Beatley enough.'" They then ran the tape through an automatic double-tracker to wobble the sound a bit. Though it went uncredited for years because of restrictive clauses in their recording contracts, Clapton composed a masterfully sorrowful underscoring of his friend's lyrics and slide guitar play. It was the first time a nonmember of the band had recorded a solo with the Beatles.

In October 1968, Harrison returned past favors by playing on Cream's last album, titled *Goodbye* in case anybody hadn't heard about their imminent breakup. A song co-written with Clapton, as Harrison told the story, had begun one day when they were fooling around with Starr at the Harrisons' estate. "The whole song was quite silly," Harrison said. Ringo was drunk and joking—he tossed out the line about the kid who was married to Mabel. (In Liverpool slang "our kid" was a catchall term for any guy, though it often referred to a little brother.) In the studio Clapton didn't start playing until the first bridge. Harrison was scribbling lyrics and had written "Bridge" to mark the song's middle. Clapton squinted at his friend's handwriting and laughed. "What's that—Badge?" The song—now known as "Badge"—became one of Cream's (and Clapton's) signature hits.

Later Harrison wrote *Abbey Road*'s "Here Comes the Sun" while a guest at Clapton's Hurtwood Edge. Their dedication to their friendship would last as long as they were on Earth together, but Pattie could clearly see how smitten Eric was with her. Sometimes she indulged the pleasure of wanting him—a flutter of fingertips on his knee as they sat talking, a touch of breast to his arm at a party as he refilled her wineglass. But she was determined to let it go no further: How could they risk their extraordinary lives?

In December 1968, Clapton was asked to join the Rolling Stones for a Christmas TV special, "Rock and Roll Circus." The lineup included Yoko Ono, the Who, and Jethro Tull. An impromptu garage band dubbed Winston Legthigh and the Dirty Mac had Clapton on lead, John Lennon on rhythm, Charlie Watts on drums, and Keith Richards on bass as Mick Jagger yowled Buddy Holly's "Peggy Sue." They made up costumes and appeared to have a great time, but Jagger pouted about his performance on seeing it played back and wouldn't let the telecast proceed. Pattie said that a few weeks after that, she and Eric were walking on London's Oxford Street. "Eric suddenly said to me, 'Do you like me, or are you seeing me because I'm famous?' I answered: 'Oh, I thought you were seeing me because *I'm* famous.'"

———

Speculation grew that Clapton would soon join the Rolling Stones as their lead guitarist. "Mick was in awe of him," said a Stones insider, "whereas Keith didn't give a fuck. One thought he was too good, the other thought he wasn't good enough." Clapton said he was very glad it didn't happen, after the Stones' catastrophic dance with the Hells Angels at Altamont. He had left Cream feeling liberated, but in a nakedly contradictory move, he jumped right back into another overhyped supergroup—and one with Ginger Baker. Clapton cooked up the new band, Blind Faith, with the immensely talented singer and keyboard player Stevie Winwood, who had recently left Traffic. They were agreeing on how much they loved *Music from Big Pink*, and suddenly they felt the need to form such a band; they went out and got Baker and bass player Rich Grech. More than 100,000 people turned out for their first concert in Hyde Park, for which they didn't have enough material, but they were proud of the album they recorded. "I think it's a lovely record," Clapton later said. "I like its looseness. It's like a supersession record, except it's got a little something more than that. You can feel there's a lot of longing in the band."

But Blind Faith did not survive the trip across the Alantic.

———

At Madison Square Garden, their concert seemed to be on the verge of self-immolation; a riot erupted when fans charged the stage trying to rip off Blind Faith souvenirs. Cops wore out their sticks on people's heads, Baker took a clubbing while trying to impose order from the stage, and Winwood's electric piano got wrecked.

Clapton had written "Presence of the Lord" because he was feeling good about himself and the new home he had made for himself at Hurtwood Edge. He said it was a song of gratitude, not a particular expression of religion. Clapton had moved from his Pheasantry home, in part, because he believed that a London cop named Norman Pilcher, who had busted Lennon and Hendrix and shaken down Jagger, had been dying to arrest him, too. Calling Pilcher "a groupie cop," Clapton later said, "I was on the run from flat to flat and when I finally got out of town the pressure was off. It was such a relief, and it was such a beautiful place that I sat down and wrote it."

With Winwood singing, Blind Faith always performed the song in the concerts, and after the Minneapolis show, two young men somehow got past security and asked Clapton to pray with them. He did, and then being the amiable young rock 'n' roller that he sometimes was, he wanted to show them his new Jimi Hendrix poster, and out instead rolled the image of Jesus! He had no idea how that got there. It must be a miracle! Since childhood, Clapton had demonstrated a tendency to obsess, and for weeks he pestered the roadies and musicians about his calling. "I ran around telling everybody I was a born-again Christian and God-knows-what," he said, embarrassed, years later. His faith proved too lukewarm to sustain.

Winwood knew that nothing miraculous was happening with that band or its tour. "The show was vulgar, crude, disgusting," he said. "It lacked integrity. There were huge crowds everywhere, full of mindless adulation, mostly due to Eric and Ginger's success with Cream and, to a more modest extent, my own impact. The combination led to a situation where we could have gone on and farted and gotten a massive reaction."

———

Before the Madison Square Garden fiasco, Clapton had noticed that the opening act was having great fun. In fact, they were blowing his headliners off the stage. Clapton knew about Delaney and Bonnie and Friends through George Harrison. On a swing through California, Harrison had gone to see them at a Hollywood bar called Snoopy's. He missed the show, but he brought back one of their records and passed it on to Clapton, saying that he was impressed.

Delaney Bramlett had spent his boyhood in Pontotoc County, Mississippi, but had been scuffling around Los Angeles trying to score a hit song since the midfifties. He was a member of the Shindogs, the house band of the rock 'n' roll TV show *Shindig* that ABC aired from 1964 to 1966 with an acne medication as the sponsor. The show's most enduring contribution to rock 'n' roll was the spectacle of go-go dancers.

Bonnie Lynn O'Farrell had grown up in a steelworker's family in the St. Louis area. Rhythm and blues clubs in the Gaslight Square section of St. Louis exposed her to Little Milton, Albert King, and Ike and Tina Turner. "When Bonnie first saw the Turners," said her friend Lorraine Rebennack, the wife of Dr. John, "she pointed to Tina, whipping her head around and shaking her ass on stage, and said, 'Baby, that's what I want to be!'"

Bonnie sang and styled well enough to become the first white member of the Ike and Tina Turner Revue. She then chased her dream west to Los Angeles, opened for the Shindogs one night in 1967, and married Delaney a week later. With short blond hair, skintight miniskirts, and a pair of green snakeskin knee boots directing attention to well-formed thighs, she was a bawdy house of fire. Delaney and Bonnie assembled a big white soul revue that generated a definite buzz on the West Coast. To some, the Bramletts were visionaries who extended white gospel-inflected rock to the horizon of soul. Others believed they were pushy mediocrities. But few questioned their ability to put on a live show that shook floors and swelled roofs with a wild good time.

After the concert in New York, Baker, Winwood, and Grech had all dashed back to England for an emotional and psychological respite. Clapton stayed on in the States and hung out with Delaney, who commiserated with the guitarist. As the tour resumed and rolled across the continent, the two struck up a close friendship. Clapton preferred the company of the Bramletts and their band to his own group and entourage. Delaney was steeped in the lore and music of Robert Johnson and other Delta blues heroes. Just talking to Bramlett helped bring Clapton back to where he wanted to be. Six years older, Bramlett became a sort of big brother and Christian drill sergeant to Clapton. He asked him why he didn't sing more with Blind Faith. The Blind Faith material didn't call for his help on vocals, Clapton told Bramlett.

And, he confessed, he really didn't think his voice was any good. Nonsense, Bramlett told him.

"No, man," said Clapton. "I can't sing."

"Yes, you can," Bramlett insisted.

Years later, on Willie Nelson's bus, Clapton would tell Atlantic producer Jerry Wexler, "Delaney taught me everything I know about singing." Bramlett informed his new protégé that he had to start writing more, too. Soon they were talking about Clapton's solo record, which Bramlett would produce with his band doing the session work. Bramlett wanted to call this album *Eric Clapton Sings*.

In the meantime, the Blind Faith tour got no better. When they played in Los Angeles, they looked out and saw a solid wall of cops in front of the stage. Fights broke out continually, and the lights were turned up so the police could make arrests. In the next-to-last concert, in Phoenix, cops bullied Clapton back to the stage area when he tried to walk out to listen to Delaney and Bonnie and Friends. For the encore, Blind Faith and the opening acts always jammed on "Sunshine of Your Love." As Bonnie shook her bootie at the foot of the Phoenix stage, a board shattered and pitched her 10 feet to a crash landing on a concrete floor. Delaney was whacked with a nightstick as he tried to get to her, and Baker was almost arrested when he rushed forth yelling at the cops. Another riot engulfed the hall. The musicians fled the stage.

Though they had one more date to play, in Honolulu in August 1969, Bonnie's spill and the mayhem that followed marked the ignominious end of Blind Faith. On his way home, Clapton stayed awhile in Los Angeles with the Bramletts because he enjoyed their company; also, there was the solo album he and Delaney were cooking up. "He's such an enthusiastic, generous character," Clapton said of his cheer-leader and mentor, "and incredibly affectionate—if he becomes your buddy he's your bosom buddy. He's also ambitious, too. A very strange combination. So, I mean, he'd sit down and write a song and tell you you'd written part of it! He'd write most of it and then say, 'Don't you remember, that's the part you put in the other day.' If you thought about it you'd realize you hadn't actually done any of it, so it was kind of like he was giving you this song and also selling himself through it at the same time."

Early in the tour with Blind Faith, Delaney had stood watching their act with their baby-faced keyboard player and backup singer, a charismatic Southerner named Bobby Whitlock. Delaney nodded at Clapton onstage and asked, "What would you think of him joining up with us?"

"Great guitar player," the youngster joked. "But we're a rock 'n' roll band. He'd have to do something about those pink silk pants." Years later, Whitlock told the story with a laugh. "Of course, it wasn't just a few months before I had me some pink silk pants myself."

3

MOVEABLE FEAST

"I COME FROM RIVER RATS, whores, and moonshiners," Bobby Whitlock jovially described his origins. He was born in Memphis on March 18, 1948, to a family that included a madam of a Lepanto, Arkansas, brothel and a 600-pound Cherokee great-grandmother called Rosie whose husband, Jake, was shot in the back by a shotgun-wielding field hand. The last words of Whitlock's great-grandfather were: "Don't shoot me anymore, Roscoe. You've already killed me." The killer, Roscoe Jacobs, answered his cry for mercy by blowing his face off. Later, Roscoe's mother cooked him a meal and doused it with poison before taking it to the jail in Osceola, because she couldn't stand to see her son hanged. The jailer took the food from her but later threw it out to the dogs, saying that a last supper for such a man was a waste of food. The dinner killed the dogs, of course, and Roscoe, who probably didn't have much appetite, dropped through the scaffold and hit the hard lariat the next morning.

The vastly obese Great-Grandma Rosie was arrested and charged as an accomplice, on suspicion that she and Roscoe were partners in a love triangle. At this time she had six small children, one of them a polio victim who was dragged through the woods and river bottoms on a skid. The authorities dismissed the charges against Rosie for lack of evidence. She subsequently remarried and died in childbirth. The casket that kin built for the woman and her stillborn infant was so big they had to remove door facings and wagon sideboards to haul it to the graveyard.

Bobby Whitlock's mother, LaVada "Bitsy" King, told that story and many more in an unpublished memoir of her family and girlhood titled *When I Left Alto*. It reads like a blend of *The Grapes of Wrath*, *Cool Hand Luke*, and the fiction of Flannery O'Connor and Cormac McCarthy. "The night I was born," she wrote, "Daddy was shacked up with some old whore across Little River. He sent a man over to get the mattress off Mama's bed. He took the mattress and left Mama to sleep on the springs. I was born on bedsprings by a black midwife. Don't you know that was bound to be miserable trying to give birth on bedsprings?"

The family was so poor during the Depression that Bobby's grandmother and scoundrel grandfather went door-to-door trying to sell shoelaces, neckties, razor blades, aspirin, and Ex-Lax. One time in Texas, where their extended family had hoped to find farm work, they ate culled grapefruit, cabbage, potatoes, and a mess of dried peas thoroughly mixed with pellets of mouse manure. Bobby's grandfather was always on the run from the law. Bitsy King wrote, "There was a Pentecostal preacher by the name of Fred Crabtree holding a meet'in'"—a revival—"in Lepanto Church of God. The church was located on the corner by the artesian well, and while he was preaching, he had Daddy and another man out stealing the congregation's chickens." Stolen chickens brought 25 cents apiece, but the arrest got her daddy sentenced to Tucker Farm, a horrific Arkansas prison where convicts who died had their legs cut off and tossed in on top of them, to conserve lumber for their pine boxes.

And that was just his mother's side of the family. "Lord-E-Me he was good-looking," LaVada said of Bobby's father, the late Jimmy Whitlock. She rued that she was just 14 when they married, and that once she realized the scope of her mistake, she did everything she could to keep from consummating it with the 18-year-old soldier. With that she cut the memoir off abruptly, choosing not to further describe the father of her children or the next 32 years of her life.

Bobby's lineage was part Cherokee, of the Golden Throat Hatchet clan. He qualified for a share of tribal land in Oklahoma; the women in his family with long straight black hair were part or all Cherokee. His description of his father's origins was enigmatic: "Daddy was born south of Hell and north of Damnation Creeks. He grew up on a farm in Mississippi. My mama gave him his first pair of store-bought shoes. Daddy worked on Mississippi River tugboats, which is a hard life. Right after I was born he had a moment"—a spiritual experience—"and dedicated his life to being a preacher. Which didn't mean he stopped drinking and drugging and abusing. Preaching just added to those things—a license to kill."

Jimmy Whitlock ministered to woebegone Southern Baptist congregations in Arkansas and Tennessee. "Daddy was a little bitty man," Bobby reminisced. "Four foot eight. He stood on two Coca-Cola crates so he could be seen behind the pulpit. But to me he was a giant, and he was a great orator. He had a sermon called 'The Devil's Quiver of Arrows.'

It was about lust and greed and sin. He'd draw back his arm and—*foom!*—let that imaginary arrow fly. I've seen deacons in the front rows duck."

The boy was terrified of his dad. "When I was 6, he was preaching way down a gravel road, somewhere outside Marmaduke, Arkansas. He had another sermon he was real proud of—'Beneath the Shade of the Old Olive Tree.' I was sitting back in church with this friend and he was preaching that one; we got the giggles. He said, 'You boys, hold it down back there.' He stopped the sermon and made us come sit on the front pew. I knew I was in trouble, but we started laughing again, couldn't help it. Daddy took me outside and beat me up like a grown man. With his fists. I was all swelled up and black and blue, but he made me come back in and sit on the front row while he finished his sermon. Everything got real quiet in there.

"After church we were going out to have Sunday dinner, elsewhere known as lunch, with members of the church, which was one of the ways of paying the preacher. I thought Ross and Lillian were rich because they had two mules *and* a tractor. Everybody was all pissed off at my dad for doing that to me. But I was thinking, 'What now?' He took me outside and put me in a corn stall of their barn. He reached up on the wall and took down a leader line that goes between the harnesses of mules. He wrapped that strap around his hand, and he beat me from head to toe. I grew up in fear. I was a grown man, with children of my own, before it dawned on me that fear is an illusion. It's not like a lion that's about to jump on you. It's just a thought."

Much of the time the preacher was away conducting

revivals or studying in seminaries while his family got by as field hands. Bobby remembered watching his mother pick cotton while dragging his baby sister on the sack between the rows. He graduated from hauling the water bucket and sharpening hoes to chopping cotton. He was still working in cotton and bean fields at 15.

But another constant in his life was music. His mother played the piano, and she could read music. His big Cherokee grandmother balanced him on her knees and sang hymns and spirituals to him while playing a Dobro. "My dad was always taking on all these falling-down little churches out in the middle of nowhere. It was his calling to resurrect them. The best thing about that was the black churches right down the road. I'd sneak out and go to the black churches and listen to all that great music." But music was no safe haven. One day Bobby was doing some chores and started singing "Swing Low, Sweet Chariot." "Daddy heard me and said, 'I want you to sing at church on Sunday.' I said, 'I'm not gonna do it.' 'Oh, yes, you are.' *Bam!* He knocked me all the way through the house."

Whitlock's mother, he said, was too cowed by the man to do anything about the abuse. Eventually he was able to halt it himself. "I caught his fist one time and was strong enough to just hold it. I told him, 'You're not gonna do that to me anymore.' Daddy tried to live up to his preaching. He did the best he could, limited by what he had to work with. But he could not get past his past."

Like millions of American kids in the 1950s, Bobby had a cheap 45-rpm record player and wore the grooves off tunes by Little Richard, Elvis, and Fats Domino. His dad groused,

"I'm trying to get everybody to heaven, and that music's going to send everybody to hell." During Whitlock's teens, the preacher suffered a breakdown and spent some time in a Veterans Administration mental hospital; Bobby was sent to stay with an aunt in Minnesota. He came back blowing on a chromatic harmonica engraved with hula dancers. He went to high school in Millington, Tennessee, a town 20 miles upriver from Memphis that owed its economy, and some notoriously rowdy honky-tonks, to a large naval air station. Along with his harp, he started playing the guitar, then the drums, then the organ. He was second chair at drums in school, but he never learned to read music, and he didn't know how he picked up instruments so quickly. He also had a cocksure singing voice and a way with words passed on to him by generations of peckerwood storytellers.

Whitlock was small but not as diminutive as his dad. With a mess of dark brown curls, he looked like some angel afloat in a Renaissance painting. He started out in a teen band called Out of It and moved on to one called the Counts. "I wasn't listening to the Beatles or the Rolling Stones. I wasn't interested. But I could sure sing 'Expressway to Your Heart.' 'Groovin'.' 'Good Lovin.' We used to play a club in Texarkana that had a big white stripe down the middle—it marked the state line of Texas and Arkansas. There were guys in blue polyester suits with lightning streaks on the sides of their shoes. Their girlfriends were all in high heels. We'd be playing 'Knock on Wood' and 'Hold On, I'm Coming,' and they were yelling, 'Why don't you play something *new* like "Kansas City"?' We gave them 'Kansas City' all night long one night."

A great many young musicians could tell variations of

that story in the 1960s. The difference for Bobby Whitlock was that he was learning his chops in Memphis, a major American music town, from players and singers who were already legends. Peter Guralnick wrote in his book *Sweet Soul Music* that Southern rhythm and blues spawned "a gospel-based, emotion-baring kind of music that grew up in the wake of the success of Ray Charles." The blues was juiced up and heartened—and given access to a white audience—by hitching a ride on the freedom train, the fight to win civil rights. (Motown, the other strain of sixties soul music, was brilliantly marketed to the same effect, but largely shied away from the politics.)

Almost every day Bobby hung out at Stax Records, which sold vinyls in a front room and had a recording studio in the back. The marquee proclaimed the establishment "Soulsville USA." His mentors Steve Cropper, a composer and rhythm guitarist, and Donald "Duck" Dunn, a bass player, had varied day jobs but were part of the Stax studio band. They were among the first white musicians to gain credibility in Memphis rhythm and blues. Cropper joined a black keyboard player and college student, Booker T. Jones, in Booker T. and the MGs. The band's 1962 instrumental "Green Onions" reached number one on *Billboard*'s rhythm and blues chart and number three among pop singles. Booker T. let Bobby watch over his shoulder when he played the organ, as long as he didn't make any noise. Dunn played bass behind Otis Redding until Redding's death in a plane crash in 1967. Cropper's writing credits included "Green Onions," Wilson Pickett's "634-5789" and Eddie Floyd's "Knock on Wood." And though Jerry Wexler and Tom Dowd asserted Atlantic's heft and technology in Redding and Pickett sessions, according to Guralnick, Cropper exercised de facto control of the Stax studio.

Supremely confident, Whitlock considered himself a vocal soloist, but he played close attention to the songwriting team of Isaac Hayes and David Porter—especially the call-and-response routine they devised in "Hold On, I'm Coming" for Sam Moore and Dave Prater, the soul champions Sam and Dave. Whitlock was a Memphis hotshot, and once he broke free of his dad—who would die of a stroke without ever completely reconciling with his son—life came at him fast. One day at Stax, Duck Dunn and Hank Crawford, an alto sax player who arranged some of Ray Charles's songs, asked Bobby if he wanted to sing with Stax's core group. "I went to the Lansley Brothers store and bought me a lime green suit with maximum gloss and collars out to *here*. First time I ever rode an airplane was going with those guys to Atlanta. I'm getting to stand out in front of Booker T. and the MGs and sing 'Knock on Wood,' 'Midnight Hour,' '634-5789.' Yeah, brother. I can sing the shit out of that."

Many nights in Memphis, Bobby's band would play one set, then Albert King would come on next." The old bluesman, who always wore a porkpie hat and sucked on a pipe when he wasn't playing, was one of Bobby's heroes—and one of his guitar riffs drives the song "Layla." "I was watching in the studio when Albert recorded 'Crosscut Saw,'" Bobby reminisced. "To the end of his days, when I ran into him he'd always tell people, 'I've known little Bobby since he could hardly look over the console.'"

Whitlock's friends at Stax decided they wanted some of the cash that white teenagers were throwing at records. They launched a sublabel called Hip Records and gave him a contract. Unfortunately, their idea of teen rock was something like Herman's Hermits. "The band was Booker T. and the MGs and the Memphis Horns," Whitlock said, "so we weren't no shabby outfit." But he wanted to wail like Al Green; he said the worst of the songs they gave him to record was "Raspberry Rug," a bit of whimsy coauthored by Leon Russell that had Bobby trying to make soul out of saccharine lines about the beauty of his dreams.

Despite Whitlock's relative success with Booker T. and the MGs, Whitlock wasn't married to Memphis or his opportunity with Stax. He *was* newly married to a young girl, but they had run off and done it on impulse; he was hardly ready to get a day job and start a family. Duck Dunn and Don Nix, a sax player and stalwart of the Memphis Horns, mentioned to Bobby one day that they had discovered a couple singing their asses off in a bowling alley in Hawthorne, California. Their scouting resulted in Stax signing Delaney and Bonnie Bramlett and recording their first album, *Home*. In late 1968, the couple came through Memphis to see how they were doing with their label. Not that well, they eventually decided—they would jump to Elektra for their second record, *Accept No Substitutes*. Bramlett was an ambitious man who knew he was on the brink of the big time, and he wanted a more powerful label. Stax couldn't have been thrilled about the disloyalty, for they'd lost money on *Home*. Nevertheless, Bobby's mentor Duck Dunn would coproduce Elektra's follow-up with Bramlett's old friend in California, the ubiquitous Leon Russell.

But before they recorded their watershed LP, they had to recruit a band. During their trip to Memphis, the Bramletts went to the Cabaret Club to see Bobby Whitlock and his band, the Counts. That night they bought him some drinks, and after talking to him for a while, they asked Whitlock if he'd like to come out to California and help them start their band. He said, "Well, yeah!" He was the first sideman they recruited. They offered him the job on a Wednesday, and by Saturday he was sleeping on their sofa in the Los Angeles suburbs. But the streetwise hotshot did have some maturity issues. "My wife!" he exclaimed. "I *forgot* that I had a wife!" The girl's parents arranged to have the marriage go away, doubtless relieved to see the young man gone.

———

Whitlock quickly saw that being his bosses' houseguest was not an ideal situation. As the band was coming together and he learned how to sing backup for the Bramletts, he found a room in a house out in Sherman Oaks. On an outlying edge of Los Angeles, the San Fernando Valley community has the soul of the quintessential American suburb. But back in the oaks and culs-de-sac, one house rocked with Dionysian abandon. The house was the soon-to-be-famous Plantation; the tenant was Leon Russell, though he kept his own quarters and studio on Skyline Drive a short distance away. Whitlock had made his generation's pilgrimage to California, only to find he was living on Tulsa Time.

Born in 1942 in Lawton, an Oklahoma army town, Leon Russell had grown up in Tulsa as Claude Russell Bridges. He formed his first band in junior high and at 14 landed his first gig playing in a Tulsa club on a bill with Ronnie Hawkins and the Hawks, whose sidemen evolved into the Band. At storied Cain's Ballroom, the youth so impressed Jerry Lee Lewis that the Killer took him out on tour. Russell went to

Will Rogers High and played organ for the choir, whose singers included another future rock star, Elvin Bishop, and Anita Bryant, a Miss America who made a career of being squeaky clean. Russell was one of those types whose image and traces show up everywhere. In the sixties and seventies he was American rock's equivalent of Gertrude Stein, whose stony gaze and wry humor tantalized writers and artists in Paris in the twenties. Russell always attracted a salon.

His hometown confounded the Dust Bowl stereotype of Oklahoma. Tulsa had the feel of an old Western city, such as St. Louis, but it was also a showcase of Art Deco architecture. Oil wealth supported a diverse music heritage. Woody Guthrie and Chet Baker had roots in that part of Oklahoma. Bob Wills first popularized his big band hybrid, western swing, in Fort Worth, behind an emcee, flour salesman, and eventual Texas governor named Pappy O'Daniel, but the reach of a 50,000-watt station, KVOO, prompted Wills to transfer his base to Tulsa in 1934. Tulsa's oil companies scheduled their employees' lunch hours so they could go to Cain's Ballroom and observe his live broadcasts. Wills had moved on by the time Russell was born, but local conjecture had it that Russell chose to go by Leon in honor of Wills's trademark call to his steel guitar player, "Take it away, Leon."

Russell lit out for Southern California as soon as he got out of high school. He connected with the producer Phil Spector and, along with guitarist Glen Campbell, drummer Hal Blaine, and bass player Carol Kaye, he became part of the Wrecking Crew, session players in continual demand in recording studios. He played piano on Jan and Dean's "Surf City" and Bobby "Boris" Pickett's "Monster Mash," and helped arrange albums by Herb Alpert and the Tijuana Brass. But Russell always had an eye out for a vehicle that would thrust him out of the background and make him a star. Russell loved being the hottest part-time resident of Tulsa. He bought an old Church of God building there and converted it into the Church Studio, which would become one of the bases of his Shelter Records and over the years, attract a range of artists from Willie Nelson to Bob Dylan. Russell hung out with the manic aspiring actor Gary Busey and built a lavish lake house outside Tulsa that was a shrine to area teenagers. A Tulsa sound and a community of avid players emerged in the sixties and early seventies, and the twang of Russell's nasal drawl personified the town's claim to being a rock 'n' roll subcapital. Most of the memorable players advanced their careers elsewhere, but they clung to a distinctive Southwestern style with strong roots in blues, gospel, and country.

Russell was loyal to old friends, and he was always trying to involve them in his schemes. Among his favorites was the bass player Carl Dean Radle. Born June 18, 1942, he was the same age as Russell and had gone to another Tulsa high school, Edison; they played some of their first gigs together. Slender and stoop-shouldered, Radle wore glasses, and his hairline was falling back fast. He struck folks as a retiring guy until he started playing an electric bass guitar. He could take over the stage in a rock number, and he had a knack for making every thrumming note stand out. "One of the most outstanding things about Carl," Russell said of Radle's style, "was his choice of notes and the choice of spaces in between. In music his taste was impeccable, and the strength of simplicity reigned supreme."

Not long after he arrived in California, Russell talked the bass player into moving to Los Angeles. Radle played gigs with Bobby Rydell and joined a group called Skip and Flip, led by Skip Battin, a future member of the Byrds. They had charted a hit in 1960 with "Cherry Pie," and with Carl in the band they recorded "Tossin' and Turnin'" and "Every Day I Have to Cry," but the leaders of the band oddly kept trying to make teen pop jive with the cha-cha. After a couple of years Radle gave up on making a living in music and returned to Tulsa, where he enlisted in the Air Force Reserve.

Through an alliance with producer Snuff Garrett, formerly a scuffling disc jockey in Texas, Russell meanwhile recognized a gold mine of opportunity in Gary Lewis—the comedian Jerry Lewis's son. Gary Lewis had received a set of drums for his 14th birthday. After 4 years of apprenticeship and a regular gig at Disneyland, Lewis landed a Liberty Records contract with Garrett as his producer. Garrett advised him to get out front and let someone else do the drumming, and he turned Lewis over for grooming to Leon Russell. Garrett and Russell urged Lewis to use his dad's connections to score a date on *The Ed Sullivan Show.* Gary Lewis and the Playboys pulled that off in January 1965, and their song "This Diamond Ring" shot to number one on the pop charts at once. Over the next 2 years, they had seven songs in the Top 10. The writer or arranger of all those songs was Leon Russell.

In 1965, Carl Radle came back home from his Air Force duty in Texas. By then the original Playboys had burned out. Russell called three friends from Tulsa—Radle, drummer Jimmy Karstein, and guitarist Tom Tripplehorn—and told them to get out to Los Angeles as fast as they could. Radle was hesitant to give the music livelihood another try, but Russell convinced him to help anchor the new Playboys. With Radle aboard, the Playboys had a stellar year, recording "Everybody Loves a Clown" and "Count Me In," and they were all over the national TV shows—*Shindig, Hullabaloo, The Tonight Show*, and a repeat on *Ed Sullivan*. But then harsh reality intervened, in the form of the Vietnam War. In late 1966, Gary Lewis got his draft notice in the mail.

Radle hung on, working behind Dobie Gray in clubs and doing session work for John Lee Hooker. He played gigs at casinos in Nevada. Ever resourceful, Russell rebounded from Gary Lewis being drafted and continued his profitable session gigs with the Wrecking Crew while keeping an eye out for another cash cow. Two years earlier, while Radle was enduring close-order drill in the Air Force, Russell had been a member of the cast of the TV show *Shindig."* Russell played piano behind the house band, the Shindogs, whose bass player was Delaney Bramlett.

When his pal married Bonnie and recorded their first album with Stax, Russell's commercial instincts perked up again. Delaney had some down-home skill and presence, especially playing the guitar, and Bonnie glowed onstage like red-hot coals. Russell offered to help produce their second album, play with them in the studio and in live gigs as often as he could, and work with them to assemble just the right band. The Bramletts came back from Memphis with the boy-wonder singer and organ player Bobby Whitlock, and not long after that, Russell called his Tulsa crony Carl Radle, who was once more about ready to give up. Russell told him to quit thinking like that and to gear up again to hit the road, cash some checks, and have a ball—this was a gig that could make them forget Gary Lewis.

Russell provided Whitlock and Radle with housing in the Plantation in Sherman Oaks while he auditioned other players and the band rehearsed. The first two Dominos, Whitlock and Radle, were allied now, waiting for the arrival of the leader called Derek.

———

Leon Russell arranged music, strategies, people's lives—he made things happen. The Tulsa cronies were just one of his circles of talented acquaintances. He also ushered into contention for Delaney and Bonnie Bramlett's band a young member of the Wrecking Crew named Jim Gordon.

He was born on New Year's Day 1945 and was the sort of American boy who seemed to exist only on TV series. Gordon had grown up in the quiet part of Sherman Oaks, just a few hills and canyons removed from the wildness of Russell's Skyline house and the Plantation. His mother was a nurse on a maternity ward, his father an accountant who went to AA meetings and coached his sons' Little League team. As described in a subsequent, spellbinding *Rolling Stone* profile by Barry Rehfeld, Gordon made his first drum set out of trash cans. He was a tubby kid, sensitive about being fat but compelled to gorge himself. Gordon had imaginary friends that he carried on conversations with, but that's not unusual. And in adolescence he shed his chubbiness and shot up tall, curly haired, and handsome, a class president in junior high and a star musician. He played with the Burbank Symphony, performed one year in the Tournament of Roses Parade, and in a competition got to tour Europe with his high school

band. While in Paris, he proposed to his sweetheart, a striking dancer named Jill.

Gordon had a chance to go to UCLA on a scholarship,
but instead he enrolled in a community college and worked
with a pickup band and fake ID at weddings and bar mitz-
vahs. A friend who played sax for Duane Eddy recommended
him for a demo, and then he got a 1963 gig playing on tour
behind the Everly Brothers. "His name was on everybody's
lips," said the Wrecking Crew's top drummer, Hal Blaine,
who called him "the only living metronome." Gordon was
the real drummer on three Monkees records—the sitcom
quartet that Hollywood hitched to the Beatles' bandwagon.
Gordon juggled sessions with the Byrds, the Righteous
Brothers, Judy Collins, Gordon Lightfoot, Bobby Darin,
and Andy Williams. He worked on Glen Campbell's break-
out version of Jimmy Webb's "Wichita Lineman" and "These
Boots Are Made for Walking" by Nancy Sinatra. Like many
women he played with, Sinatra was crazy about him.

Jim and Jill soon had a Mercedes 220S, a mortgaged home
in North Hollywood, and a child. Gordon's Wrecking Crew
colleague Carol Kaye, who pioneered recorded music's shift
from the stand-up bass to the electric bass guitar, was with
them at the hospital the night their daughter was born. "Jim
was the sweetest guy," said Kaye. "An All-American boy."

As if that weren't enough fast-track opportunity, Jim and
Jill both landed jobs on *Shindig,* where he played with Delaney Bramlett and she danced with Teri Garr. Gordon already
knew Leon Russell from the studio sessions, and the exposure
to the big-name rock stars parading through the TV cast
whetted his appetite for the thrill of a life in music that did not
resemble going to the office. Gordon's efforts to lead his own

group bore indifferent fruit, with the band making one record and lasting just a year, and his storybook marriage began to unravel. He spent more and more time hanging out with a willowy backup singer that Russell brought into Delaney and Bonnie Bramlett's soul revue, Rita Coolidge.

The Bramletts and Russell meanwhile recruited a fine English lead guitarist, Dave Mason, who had left the band Traffic, and a top horn section with Bobby Keys on tenor sax and Jim Price on trumpet, both of whom were later snatched up by the Rolling Stones. At the debut concert for Delaney and Bonnie and Friends' 1969 album *Accept No Substitute*, Russell wore a white tux and top hat and played a white grand piano. The act was a hot commodity built around a volatile marriage. George Harrison passed through Hollywood hoping to hear them, and back in England he passed their record to Eric Clapton.

The Bramletts' original drummer, Russell's Tulsa chum Jim Keltner, was also part of the Wrecking Crew. Like Hal Blaine and Carol Kaye, Keltner thought a great deal of Jim Gordon. Keltner was ambivalent about life on the road, and the Bramletts were astir with plans for a tour across America with Blind Faith, after which they wanted to storm England and make other stops in Europe. Keltner told *Rolling Stone,* "He traded me some studio gigs for a chance to work with Delaney and Bonnie. He became the main guy because he was better." The band leaders were delighted with this athlete of a drummer with the movie star looks. Bonnie Bramlett said, "He was gentle, sincere, considerate, brutally handsome, charming as a snake, and could he play! He was right on the money. I could do whatever I wanted. I was really enjoying myself. We all were. And it showed."

But Jill Gordon wasn't about to go on the road with a rock 'n' roll band and a small daughter, and it couldn't have helped matters at home that her husband was itching to go to Europe with his fast friend Rita Coolidge. That was the end of Jim and Jill's marriage. It had lasted 5 years.

Leon Russell had recorded just one album, *Look Inside the Asylum Choir*, with a youngster from Dallas, Marc Benno, but he thrived in Los Angeles, roaming the Hollywood hills in a Rolls Royce. In Sherman Oaks, Russell provided lodging and a creative environment to musicians, many of whom were from Tulsa. J. J. Cale holed up in the garage apartment writing love songs like "Crazy Mama" to a flame in Atlanta. Jesse Ed Davis, a Kiowa guitarist from Oklahoma they called "Indian Ed," brought around bluesman Taj Mahal, who lived nearby. Bobby Whitlock had great rapport with the bass player, Carl Radle, who was 5 years older. Radle treated him with the consideration of an older brother. He nicknamed Whitlock the strawberry alarm clock because he was always up so early, making some kind of racket. He said he never would have known anything about his surroundings if not for Radle, who let him ride his Triumph motorcycle. He roamed on winding blacktops through brush with the overpowering scent of licorice, along tall roadside sentinels of eucalyptus, and took in the magical overlook of the Pacific at Malibu.

The Plantation swarmed with hookers, topless dancers, and groupies wolfing down quaaludes. Whitlock was upstairs when a couple of guys got in a squabble over a hooker, and one pulled a pistol and fired a wild shot. Russell wrote and recorded a song about the embellished event called "Shoot Out on the Plantation." Whitlock was relatively young compared with the rest of Russell's wild bunch, and he was sometimes treated like a kid. For company he adopted a cat and a little mongrel dog. Radle's friend Jimmy Karstein, a Tulsa native and the Shindogs' former drummer, announced one day that Bobby couldn't have those animals in such a crowded place. There was no use arguing—the pets had to go. Delaney Bramlett's mother agreed to take the cat. While Bobby was driving a borrowed car to hand the scared animal to Bramlett's mother, the cat freaked out and doused Whitlock with excrement, then cowered in the package tray. Whitlock was stuck in a freeway traffic jam in a stinking car, stripped down to his underwear. He never saw his cat again after that day, and when he got back to the Plantation he found that his dog was gone as well. "Well, that's been taken care of," he claimed Karstein said.

Incensed, Whitlock was inclined to go after the drummer with fists flailing, but instead he closed the door, sat down on his bed, and fighting back tears and fury, he picked up his guitar. Whitlock, who had a passion for horticulture, described his jumble of emotions: "My life then was a very small garden. Very small. And Jimmy, it came to me, was the thorn tree in my garden."

Though he'd grown up singing, the composition that poured out of him was only the second song he had written. It would resonate for a generation as the brokenhearted last call of *Layla and Other Assorted Love Songs.*

After a while he called out to Karstein. "Hey, Jimmy. Can you come in here? I'd like you to listen to this song." He sang it softly, high in his throat. "Thorn Tree in the Garden" was about a boy pining over a lost love, knowing in his heart-break that he'd never see her again, trying to imagine whom she might be loving now, wondering if he had nobody but himself to blame.

Karstein was moved, like everyone else who heard it. "God, Bobby. What a pretty song."

"Well, I just wanted you to hear it. Because someday I'm going to record it, and every time you hear it you're going to feel really bad, because you'll remember what you did to my dog."

4

SMOKIN'

CHRISTMAS MUST NEVER HAVE BEEN a happy time for Duane Allman.

His dad, Willis Allman, was born in 1918 to a family that owned a small farm about 40 miles west of Nashville. In addition to the field work, Willis's father took odd jobs to bring a little more food to the table. Music was an interim of escape and pleasure for the clan. The family would gather around the radio and listen to broadcasts of the Grand Ole Opry, and many nights the family band would pull out their instruments and perform gospel and bluegrass. Hillbilly, their music was called back then.

One of the preferred ways for young men to escape failing farms and soup lines was to join the army. But in the small American force of the thirties, it was hard to win a spot. Willis Allman flunked his first army physical because he had a hernia; his dad sold off a few acres of their land to pay for corrective surgery. Willis tried again a few months later and was told he didn't weigh enough. Back home, he stuffed himself with starches, fat, and bananas. Finally, in 1937, he was sworn in to the army. His younger brother Howard was lucky enough to join up, too, and they were assigned to the same unit. Willis Allman was a gung-ho soldier—the brass liked him and made him a roving recruiter. In Rocky Mount, North Carolina, he struck up a romance with a blonde secretary named Geraldine Robbins. Soon after they married, the Japanese bombed Pearl Harbor.

Those Allman brothers fought all over Europe and stormed the beaches of Normandy on D-day. Encouraged to re-enlist, the Allman brothers were sent home to Nashville as a team of recruiters. Willis was able to buy a comfortable house on a tree-lined street west of downtown, and he and Geraldine started a family. Their first son was born November 20, 1946. They named him Howard Duane in honor of his bachelor uncle, who lived with the family. Their second son, Gregg Lenoir, was born 13 months later.

When Willis was offered a commission, he naturally accepted. In 1949 the army sent him and his young family to Port Story, on the outskirts of Norfolk, Virginia, where they lived on base. As related in Scott Freeman's book *Midnight Riders,* Willis would call home from work and laugh as Duane burbled on the phone. The little boy hugged his daddy's leg and begged to be taken to the Officers' Club. A first lieutenant at 31, Willis Allman showed every sign of being a lifer.

He drew duty on Christmas week in 1949. Geraldine took the boys to Rocky Mount for the holiday with her family. The day after Christmas, Willis stood watch and afterward caught a ride into Norfolk with his best friend on post, a second lieutenant named Robert Buchanan. They went to a bar called the Oriental Gardens, drank some beers, and played shuffleboard. One of the challengers of the table was an out-of-work plumber's helper and combat veteran named Michael Robert Green. They drank some more, swapped war stories, and headed to a different bar. When the lieutenants decided to call it a night, Green asked if they'd give him a lift to another bar. Buchanan told him to get in.

They hadn't gone far when Green jammed a .32 calibar pistol against the back of Buchanan's head. A robbery that netted Green $4.85 turned into a ride of terror. Green made Buchanan turn off in a soaked cornfield, then he ordered the two men out of the car and told them to walk. Willis whispered to his friend to break and run one way, and he'd go the other. The gunman saw what they were planning and made them lie facedown in the mud. In desperation Willis Allman rose up and lunged for the gun. Green fired at Allman. Buchanan, whose life had just been saved, lurched to his feet and ran, and he glimpsed his friend running in another direction. As Buchanan fled, he heard more shots. He got to a phone and called for help, then raced back to search for his buddy. Buchanan found him in the cornfield, dead from a slug fired at point-blank range that had gone in under his armpit.

The night after Christmas, Geraldine Allman took the call telling her she was a widow. Her sons were 4 and 2. In a Virginia courtroom in 1951, Green testified that he didn't remember firing those shots. He was convicted of the lieutenant's murder and given the death penalty, but the day before he was to be strapped in the electric chair, governor John S. Battle commuted his sentence to life, saying that his combat in World War II had left him deranged.

Every year, on Christmas, the boys' Uncle Howard wrote

the authorities in Virginia to make sure Green was still in prison. That went on till 1975, when Green was released. He had spent 24 of his 52 years locked up for murdering another man for no reason at all.

If their dad had just gone home that night, the Allman brothers would likely have come into their teens as army brats, shuffled from one school and town and post to another. But that Christmas yanked their lives upside down, and any appeal that the military held for them soon vanished.

Geraldine and her boys moved in with Willis's parents, and she found work in an auto parts shop in Nashville, but that was no life, she decided. Geraldine was educated and resourceful enough to go to college. She found that her husband's veteran benefits would help with the cost of her education—and she could get a break on tuition and other costs if her sons went to a military school. She enrolled them in the Castle Heights Military Academy in Lebanon, Tennessee. One day she dropped them off with their suitcases and, after many tears and promises, she just drove away.

Lebanon is a town where Union and Confederate soldiers battled in the streets and where during the Second World War, George Patton directed maneuvers on the campus of a local college. The Castle Heights Military Academy echoed that tradition. Gregg recalled that time: "I thought, 'Lord, what have I done to get thrown in this place?' Get to go home three times a year. Days seemed like weeks and there were fights nearly every morning when you woke up."

Geraldine Allman stuck it out. She graduated from college, and in 1957 she rescued her sons and took them to Daytona

----

Beach. An accountant, she moved them into a house shaded by palm trees just a few blocks from the Atlantic Ocean. The brothers spent days hitting on bronzed tourist girls in bikinis who smelled of coconut oil.

Duane had emerged from the shadow of his dad's murder and the harsh experience of military school with a James Dean haircut, a give-a-shit look in his eye, and a smart mouth. Though he was a small, thin kid, his charisma was such that when he walked in a room, it was as if somebody flipped on the lights. The current that flowed was not always affection— his first friend in town was an older pool hall denizen named Jim Shepley. Initially, Shepley said, nobody much liked the guy. "He had a cocky attitude and was an aggressive type."

Duane was skipping school at Seabreeze High and giving the teachers hell when he was there. That fall of 1960, he spent the first money he ever had on a Harley 165. About that time, Gregg took the $21 profit from his first paper route and pestered a Sears, Roebuck salesman until the man finally gave him a buck's break on the price and let him walk out of the store with an electric Silvertone guitar. Duane would go in Gregg's room and fool with his guitar. "Stay out of my stuff," Gregg shouted. When Duane wrecked his Harley too badly to repair, he sold enough salvaged parts to buy his own Silvertone guitar.

During the summer they always spent time with their grandparents in Tennessee. Their grandmother would take them to the Ryman Auditorium to hear the Grand Ole Opry. But that summer, knowing about their fascination with electric guitars, she let them go to a rhythm and blues show that played to a black audience throbbing with laughter and jive. Otis Redding, Patti LaBelle, and B. B. King opened for

55

Jackie Wilson. Midway through the show Duane gaped at his little brother and said, "Man, Gregory, what have we got here? We got to get into this."

Shepley had more experience playing the guitar, and he showed them tricks employed by Lightnin' Hopkins, John Lee Hooker, and Muddy Waters. "The cat that actually taught me to play is Jim Shepley," Duane would carry on in one of his most effusive interviews. "Ol' Lightnin' Fingers, the first, number one, taking-care-of-business man in Daytona Beach, Florida. . . . The baddest cat. A very influential cat in my life, also. He's dynamite. The smokin'-est cat. I can't even talk about him, he's so hip. He glows in the dark."

Duane's academic career was over by the time he started high school. He was going to be a rock 'n' roll guitar player, end of story. Neighbors winced at the constant amplified yowling emanating from the Allmans' house. Fearful that Gregg was going to join his brother as a high school dropout, Geraldine shipped him back to the Castle Heights Military Academy for his sophomore year in 1962, a bitter blow. But as soon as Gregg came back, the guitar-playing brothers joined the House Rockers—the white backup band for a black group called the Untils. "We were a smokin' band," Duane recalled. "Boy, I mean we would set fire to a building in a second. We were just up there blowing as funky as we pleased. Sixteen years old, $41 a week. Big time."

One night at a ballpark in 1965, an Allman Brothers–led band called the Escorts got to open for the Beach Boys. They wore matching suits and ties and had haircuts like the Beatles. By the time Gregg graduated from Seabreeze High, the brothers were calling themselves the Allman Joys, a takeoff on the name of the Almond Joy candy bar. Despite their rhythm and blues roots, they wore Beatle boots and black Nehru jackets and sported haircuts like the Liverpool four. In addition to rhythm guitar, Gregg started playing a Vox stand-up organ—the rage of the British bands—and later became a fine piano player. And though he was still an amateur, he was developing a strong and memorable baritone voice.

Gregg aspired to go to college and eventually become a dentist, but Duane wanted to hit the road. The band loaded everything in an old station wagon, and soon they were playing 7 nights a week at small clubs and fraternity parties all over the Southeast. They rolled on, gaining steam and reputation, but Gregg had passed up enrolling in college that first semester after high school, and he turned 18 in December 1965. Duane was excused from Vietnam because he was the oldest surviving son of an officer who had died while on active duty. His little brother was badly in need of a draft exemption.

According to accounts that included Gregg's own story, the band leader proposed that the night before Gregg was to report for his physical, they would have a "foot-shootin' party." There were fellow musicians and lots of girls and bottles of whiskey—and a loaded Saturday night special. Gregg painted a target on his moccasin, having no desire to cripple himself. As the soused girls commenced weeping, Gregg recalled: "I took aim and I thought: 'Wait a minute, what am I doing here? I'm getting ready to shoot myself.' So I went back in and said, 'Look, I gotta have a couple more drinks before I do this.'"

SMOKIN'

Duane badgered him, questioned his manhood. "I invited these nice ladies over here to see a foot shootin', and you're going to let them down?"

Another teenage musician, Sylvan Wells, said that Gregg knocked down another couple of shots, stumbled inside, made a phone call, and came back out with the pistol. "The next thing I know is *bang!*" Wells recalled. "Then the ambulance was there; he'd called the ambulance before he shot himself." An emergency room doc was alleged to have taken note of the target painted on the boy's blood-soaked moccasin, yanked it off without compassion, cleaned and bandaged the wound, and curtly sent him on his way. But the party and the gun got him off the hook: Gregg Allman was never drafted, and he didn't walk with a limp either.

Buddy Killen, a Nashville music publisher and session player who discovered the popular rhythm and blues singer Joe Tex, recorded some Allman Joys material for a small label and released one single, an atrocious psychedelic take on Willie Dixon's "Spoonful." (Across the Atlantic, a band called Cream was meanwhile making a rock anthem of the old blues song.) Killen then broke the Allman Joys' hearts, advising them to get day jobs. Even Duane grew discouraged. "There's a garbage circuit of the South, man," he said. "You make about $150 a week and eat pills and drink. It was killing us."

With a new drummer and bass player, the band re-formed as Hour Glass. In March 1967, a band member chanced to run into some friendly guys carrying guitar cases in the St. Louis airport and invited them to watch Hour Glass that night. The Nitty Gritty Dirt Band was a group of hippie-bluegrass-country-rockers from Los Angeles. They were already on a hot streak, and 3 years later, in 1970, their cover of Jerry Jeff Walker's "Mr. Bojangles" would make them full-blown stars. The Californians were greatly impressed by this Southern soul band driven by two brothers who looked like twins. After watching Hour Glass, the Dirt Band's manager called executives at Liberty and swore he had just found them the next Rolling Stones.

"Duane, that's a jive lick," Gregg fretted about the record deal, which required them to move to Los Angeles. "Let's don't do it." But Duane was the band's leader, and at his insistence they hauled their instruments out West. In their first gig, Hour Glass opened for the Doors. Duane ended their finale with a prolonged, deafening feedback screech, and then unplugged his guitar, flung it high and tumbling end over end, and walked off the stage without a backward glance as it crashed to the floor. But Liberty had signed them because of Gregg's singing ability, not the play or showmanship of Duane. Some executive suggested that since they were Southerners, maybe the desired sound was Motown, which, of course, was rooted in Detroit. *Hour Glass,* their debut album came out in 1967. Their producers really had no idea what kind of band they were.

But the Allmans' shows at Whisky a Go Go were packed, and their jams were magnetic. A band member claimed that one night they had Buddy Miles, Paul Butterfield, Stephen Stills, Neil Young, Eric Burdon, and Janis Joplin all sitting in with them at once. In April 1968, the band tried to rescue their recording prospects by buying $500 worth of time at the Fame Recording Studios in Muscle Shoals, Alabama. Their choice of the little cinder block studio in Alabama was imbued with hopeful superstition; Percy Sledge recorded "When a Man Loves a Woman" in Muscle Shoals in 1966, and it was the first soul song to reach number one on the pop charts. With a medley of covered songs by B. B. King and John Lee Hooker, Hour Glass hoped they might catch Sledge's magic and convey their sound and purpose to their masters in Los Angeles. Capturing even the bitten-off inflection of B. B. King's speech, Gregg sounded so much like his blues hero that it was eerie. But word came back from Liberty that the tape was terrible. The Muscle Shoals investment was a waste of money, travel, and time.

For their second album, *Power of Love*, in 1968, Neil Young provided liner notes that were "witnessed" by Stephen Stills. Like the prior record, it would sink without a trace. The low point, one critic claimed, was an instrumental cover of "Norwegian Wood" with Duane plunking an electric sitar. But Bob Simmons, a popular deejay at KPFA in Berkeley, was an operating partner of the famed Avalon Ballroom in San Francisco; he remembers a February 1969 gig in which the band, who were billing themselves again as the Allman Joys, were the first of three acts headlined by the Steve Miller Band. The group that played first, as the evening's customers were just beginning to arrive, was usually a road band with low marquee value. Simmons recalls, "The band wasn't much to look at, but who was in those days? I remember the usual floral shirts and bell bottoms, and a couple of blond guys, really blond. They opened with a song, 'Power of Love,' and I stood there transfixed. I could not believe how good they were. They looked as spaced as everyone else, but they were tight, in tune, and played their asses off."

Simmons later started playing that song he heard at the

Avalon as one of his "Slipped Disks"—songs that had unaccountably fallen through the cracks. "'Power of Love' was just one of those great songs," he said, "and they had to work pretty hard to keep it from becoming a hit, but leave it to Liberty, they found a way."

The Southerners were honored and scorned simultaneously, and they were piled up like refugees in a succession of dreary Los Angeles motels. Duane was yelling, "Fuck this whole thing." They pulled out and went back to Florida and gigs in clubs where the crowds hollered, "'Mustang Sally!'"

The Allman brothers wound up in Jacksonville, where they were hired as sidemen by their friend Butch Trucks, who planned to record an album with a band he called 31st of February. Then Gregg got a stern call from someone at Liberty Records, telling him that if he didn't get his ass back to California, they were going to sue him for $48,000, which the band allegedly owed the company. They didn't ask him to bring his brother and friends along. Gregg snapped to and took off, which in Trucks's mind killed 31st of February and his record. It soured their friendship for a while.

Duane was in need of bucks and didn't know where they might come from. Then one day he got a completely unexpected call: Rick Hall, the owner of Fame Recording Studios, had witnessed those Hour Glass sessions and was impressed with Duane. He wondered if Duane would be interested in coming back to Muscle Shoals to help make a record with Wilson Pickett, Mr. Mustang Sally himself.

Bottleneck evolved as the poor black man's slide guitar. The term was at first literal: The neck of a broken wine bottle fit over the ring or middle finger of a player's hand; rubbed over the frets and along the strings of a guitar, the glass made a resonant and fluid connection of notes that the pressure of fingertips couldn't manage. You might also do it with a closed penknife, a metal cylinder, or, in Duane Allman's case, a container of Coricidin cold medicine. But playing bottleneck is hardly easy, because the sweet spot is a continually moving target. Allman had listened to recordings of Ry Cooder and Jeff Beck playing bottleneck, and in Los Angeles he was inspired by seeing a performance of "Statesboro Blues" by Taj Mahal and his guitarist, Jesse Ed Davis.

For 2 years, Allman labored at picking up the tricks of those contemporaries and predecessors such as Robert Johnson, Muddy Waters, and Elmore James. "I got me a bottleneck and went around the house for about 3 weeks saying, 'Hey, man, we've got to learn these songs—the blues to play on the stage. I love this. This is a gas.' So we started doing it. For a while, everybody would look at me, thinking, 'Oh, no! He's getting ready to do it again!' And everybody would just lower their heads—as if to say, 'Get it over with—quick.'" When Duane was learning, his bottleneck play was as soothing to his bandmates' ears as a dentist's drill. "Have you ever heard somebody trying to learn slide?" one griped. "There's nothing worse. Unless it's a fiddle player."

Despite his eventual mastery of bottleneck and finesse with other styles of blues-oriented electric guitar, Duane Allman had no gigs and no band when he got his chance as a session player. Muscle Shoals was a backwater town in northern Alabama, but because of the gifted players who thronged the Fame Recording Studios, Atlantic partner and producer Jerry Wexler counted Muscle Shoals as a base of his empire.

Wexler was impressed by Fame's past history with Joe Tex, Clarence Carter, Etta James, and Percy Sledge. The Atlantic executive sent Wilson Pickett over from Memphis to record with the now-famous Muscle Shoals Rhythm Section. But as skillful as the core sidemen were at Muscle Shoals, they were all horns and rhythm—they didn't have a good guitar player.

Duane Allman was broke and just 20 years old, but he wasn't cowed by anyone. Accounts differ on what exactly was said when the hippie sauntered into the studio, plugged in his Stratocaster and Fender Twin amplifier, and started challenging Pickett to record "Hey Jude." Some thought Pickett had misheard the title from Paul McCartney's vocal as "Hey Jew," and that his aversion was anti-Semitic. According to Rick Hall, the founder of the Fame studio and label, Pickett just said, "You guys must be crazy. I can't do that, man, that's not my bag." But Duane started in on him in the same way he'd ragged Gregg 3 years earlier at the foot-shootin' party: "What's wrong, you don't got the balls to sing it?"

Pickett had a violent temper and a huge ego. But something made him respond to Allman's impertinent challenge.

Wexler, among others, said that Allman's play on the song was what Bach and Handel called an obbligato—a part so essential that the composition would implode if it were omitted. Allman's initial presence on the cut was subtle and restrained, like a brush of watercolor dabbed here and there. When the song reached its climax, Pickett's scream and the simultaneous blast of horns would have left many guitarists hunkered down, waiting for another number. But for 50 seconds, Allman tore into it as fast as Clapton or Hendrix or the great Chicago bluesmen on their best days. Everyone who witnessed that take in the little Alabama studio seemed to know what had just occurred.

Pickett's take on "Hey Jude" would sell more than a million copies, even though it was up against the Beatles' original. In the process, Duane Allman had walked into the Fame Recording Studios a nobody and come out famous. In Memphis, Phil Walden, who had been Otis Redding's manager, called in his black assistant and played him the tape. Twiggs Lyndon had been a road manager for Little Richard and Sledge—he had been on the bus when Hendrix was in Little Richard's band. He was a hard man to snow.

"What do you think of that guitar player?" Walden asked him.

"Man, he is great," replied Lyndon, grinning.

Walden said, "He's white."

"No!" cried the music veteran. "He *can't* be."

Pickett started calling Allman "Skyman" because he was so cheerful (and was high all the time). Duane had another nickname, "Dog," which melded into "Skydog." After the session Hall implored his prize guitarist to go back to Florida, pack up, and move to Muscle Shoals. Allman lived in a cabin on a lake and drove around those Alabama woods, which were well-known Klan territory, in an old milk truck. His new patrons gave him a salary and a sterling run of first-rate session work. He gave his guitar and Coricidin bottle a Chicago-style joy ride on Clarence Carter's "The Road of Love," and in New York, Wexler put Allman to work on two of Aretha Franklin's albums, *Soul '69* and *This Girl's in Love with You*. Wexler said in his autobiography, written with David Ritz, that Allman's greatest gift was his versatility.

"He played no-bullshit blues, and he phrased like the authentic black guitarists, weaving melodic segments like elaborate tapestries. His chops were huge."

When Ry Cooder was unavailable for a session with Delaney and Bonnie Bramlett, who were then among Wexler's favorite clients, the Atlantic executive recommended Duane as a bottleneck player. Delaney was wary, believing that if Duane were any good he would have known about him, but once they got together they were instant soul brothers. Duane returned to electric sitar behind King Curtis on "Games People Play," which won a 1969 Grammy for the best rhythm and blues instrumental. For a while, Allman and Bramlett shared a pad in New York and jammed the nights away with Curtis. The great sax player of 96th Street would be stabbed to death on his stoop a few months later by a street bum. Allman sobbed inconsolably at his funeral. Duane also hung out with the soul revue band Delaney and Bonnie were assembling in California. As he did with Gregg, Allman called Bobby Whitlock "little brother."

Duane played on records by John Hammond, Ronnie Hawkins, Otis Rush, and Herbie Mann. Another high point was Boz Scaggs' first album. One of Allman's loveliest bottleneck explorations was on Scaggs' 13-minute "Loan Me a Dime." He played Dobro on the old Jimmie Rodgers country song, "Waiting for a Train," and he unveiled an uncanny trick of making an acoustic guitar chirp like a bird.

———

Duane Allman had the aura of a budding star, but one of an unusual kind. Unlike Eric Clapton, he didn't write songs, and he really did have a lousy voice. "I would like to try to sing," he told a writer once, "but the cats in my band insist I cannot sing a note. I sing around the street until I get around them, and then it just kind of dies off—they look at me hard." In Muscle Shoals, Rick Hall urged Allman to give it a try after all his fine session work, and he eagerly jumped in. They recorded a few tracks in Alabama for a proposed solo album, but his singing came off as if he was trying to be one of the rockabilly novelty acts that surfaced from time to time. Nobody had to tell him he sounded like a garage-band dreamer. Still, Wexler thought so much of his guitar playing that he bought the contract and master tapes for a modest sum—to the joy of Hall. Wexler assigned development of "the Allman band" to Phil Walden and a new sublabel, Capricorn. Walden, who had been Otis Redding's manager, said, "I swore I'd never get so involved with another artist. Then Duane Allman came along."

Walden, a curly-haired man who looked like a small-town furniture salesman, had built one of the most successful agencies in rhythm and blues, counting among his clients Sam and Dave, Percy Sledge, Joe Tex, Clarence Carter, and Otis Redding. But then Redding went down in a plane, and Walden's agency evaporated; Duane Allman represented Walden's best chance to rebuild his business, and he ran with the opportunity. Walden told Duane to go find the band he wanted. In early 1969, Allman roamed the South until he had them. First, Allman recruited the black drummer and jazz enthusiast Jaimoe Johanson; he then added a second drummer, Butch Trucks, his old friend in Jacksonville. Allman brought bass player Berry Oakley and second guitarist Dickey Betts into the fold next. In Jacksonville, they jammed for 5 days in a park and crashed on Trucks's floor. "This is *it*," Duane said of the two-lead-guitar sound that would become the band's imprint on rock 'n' roll. Betts described how they adapted their style from the model of rhythm and blues: "We used our guitars like a brass section, playing all those harmony lines. Harmonies that sounded like they took a month to write were actually improvised. It was musical telepathy."

Although the band was coming together nicely, Duane knew that the missing ingredient was his little brother, but Gregg was mired in Los Angeles, selling songs cheap to Liberty and getting high. The night after the new ensemble's breakthrough jam, Duane got on the phone and told Gregg that he had to come back *now.* Leaving behind a serious bout of depression and the unpaid debts to Liberty, he "caught the first thing smokin' toward Jacksonville." The Allman Brothers were finally a band worthy of the name.

———

There was one hitch in the deal with Phil Walden and Capricorn. Walden lived in Macon, Georgia, and he said he had to have the band there, too. Macon was an antebellum town with a chamber of commerce that bragged it had more churches per capita than any other American city; still, it was home to only 120,000 people. The Allman Brothers Band, which won fame as the big rock band from the little town in Georgia, arrived there with distinct misgivings. They settled in the town, spreading out from a central hippie crash pad into apartments and little rental houses where some band members had wives or girlfriends. They attracted a coterie of groupies from the small college in Macon. They found soul food joints that suited their appetites. But they were isolated enough that they spent a lot of their evenings in a cemetery playing guitars, passing joints, and drinking Ripple wine. Georgians, among them the governor and future president Jimmy Carter, embraced them because they were Southerners with an integrated band that could do "Whipping Post," a song drawn from the raw past of slavery, and not sound phony. But the music scene in Macon consisted entirely of them.

In Muscle Shoals, Duane had taken up with a slender blonde named Donna. She was pregnant with his daughter when they moved to Macon, but settling down did not jibe with Allman's view of himself and his future. Donna and Duane broke up, and he started living with a girl named Dixie Lee. Still, the plan was for them not to be anywhere very long. Whatever their home base, they were a road band, a constantly working band—their Capricorn debut, *Beginnings*, won some critical notice, but gigs were how they made their money.

The band rolled across the country in a Winnebago, playing 5 days a week. They were creatures of the times, and living the life: weed, psilocybin, speed, tar opium, heroin, and cocaine, the band favorite. In less than 2 years, the Allman Brothers played about 500 club dates or concerts. Twiggs Lyndon, the 27-year-old road manager, had been totally devoted to Duane Allman since Phil Walden first played him the tape of Wilson Pickett's cover of "Hey Jude." Lyndon kept the operation moving. At the end of April 1970, they drove all night to play a gig at Alliota's Lounge in Buffalo, New York. The owner, Angelo Alliota, told them they had to play two shows, and they did, though they were exhausted. But when they went back to get paid the next day, Alliota told them they had to play another show, because the night before they had shown up 15 minutes late. They sent Twiggs over to take care of the guy, and the problem.

As Scott Freeman reconstructed the episode from court records and press coverage in his book *Midnight Riders,* Twiggs's solution was to go in the bar with a 10-inch fishing knife and jump on the 55-year-old New Yorker. "I cut him," said Lyndon, when others in the entourage pulled him off. Indeed he had—once in the arm and twice, deeply, in the abdomen. Alliota died 1 hour later. Mortified, the Allman Brothers Band put up money for the best defense lawyer who could be found, but then rolled on toward the next gig. Seventeen months later, Lyndon would stand trial in Buffalo for first-degree murder. After seeing and hearing the parade of witnesses the defense lawyer produced, the jury acquitted Lyndon (who would later die when he went skydiving and his parachute failed to open) on the rationale that anyone who worked on the road with the Allman Brothers Band *had* to be insane.

5

CROSSROADS

AFTER THE BLIND FAITH TOUR whimpered to a close, Eric Clapton savored being on his native soil. He was settling into his new digs at Hurtwood Edge. The sprawling place needed a lot of work, and he had his usual number of romantic irons in the fire. A London model named Cathy James enjoyed some continuing favor. Alice Ormsby-Gore moved in with him in the spring of 1969. She left the next month, but a year later she returned. Though they had their estrangements, she would be with Clapton for most of the next 4 years. For a while Clapton was also involved with Paula Boyd, Pattie's younger sister. Clapton spoke of his relationships with an authorized biographer, Ray Coleman, starting with Alice, the ambassador's daughter: "Although we had some good times together, I'd never describe it as head over heels in love. All the time I was with Alice, I was mentally with Pattie." Paula, he went on, was "a surrogate Pattie in my mind."

Clapton and the Harrisons spent ever more time together as the Beatles grew distant from each other and the breakup seemed imminent. Paul McCartney and Ringo Starr hated John Lennon's inclusion of Yoko Ono as an artistic force in the band, and earlier that year George and Paul had almost come to blows when Paul presumed to lecture him about how to play the guitar. "That's it, see you 'round the clubs," George had snapped at Paul in storming out. The Beatles' conflict continued without resolution through 1969, with Paul emerging at one point to say that, contrary to the worldwide rumors, he was *not* dead, but that the band was. Clapton played music with George in their Surrey retreats and commiserated. Eric and Pattie carried on intense conversations for hours at a time.

One of George's enthusiasms during that year was Delaney and Bonnie and Friends, especially after the band settled in to rehearse for their European tour as guests of Clapton at Hurtwood Edge. Despite all the money that had come his way, Clapton felt burned out by his experience with both Cream and Blind Faith, and his disgust with the star charade was deepened by observing and listening to George's unhappiness with the Beatles. Clapton engaged in an impossible conceit. The moody prima donna who had reclined onstage with Cream and watched a chain elevate his squawking guitar, as if toward heaven, was now going to be just a journeyman player in an up-and-coming band. The publicity photo for *Delaney and Bonnie and Friends On Tour with Eric Clapton* would show him tramping across rough terrain with his mates, carrying his guitar case as his grandfather might have carried his toolbox or lunch pail. Gone were Clapton's permed hairdo and paisley shirt and scarf—just boots, jeans, and leather coat, straight shoulder-length hair, and a short beard. In the photo, Bobby Whitlock strode forth as a cocky and stylish kid, followed by a dog and the tall, straight-looking Jim Gordon in a blue denim jacket.

With short receding hair and a mustache, Carl Radle was characteristically partially hidden by Delaney. Derek and the Dominos had unwittingly formed and were about to make a record together, though the Bramletts tried to make clear that this was their show—their time.

Clapton was rebelling against the pop world's perception of him, and in his mind he was getting back to his roots. He remembered how much fun this band seemed to have while opening for him in the otherwise wretched Blind Faith tour of North America. Sometimes he would join them onstage batting on a tambourine, infusing himself with a bit of their energy and enjoyment. "I joined Delaney's band," Clapton said, "because I was in total awe of him, and I thought everyone *else* should see this. I knew I had the drawing power, even then. I could make the public aware of them just by putting my name on the bill."

It's significant that he always referred to the group as *Delaney's* band. His relationship with Bonnie was complicated and soon became more so. Crowds in Germany booed the act, believing they had bought tickets for a Clapton show. Clapton's manager, Robert Stigwood, was alarmed by the uncommercial behavior of his star and the widely reported booing in Frankfurt, Hamburg, and Cologne. Sent to Hurtwood Edge by Stigwood to assess the situation and build a public relations strategy, Roy Connally, a London reporter and publicist, found a scene he described as "unnerving." He said that in early evening, the mansion was dark as a set for a vampire movie, and the occupants were so stoned that no one seemed to notice that the house was an unsightly mess. Connally sensed an "air of tension beneath the shared bonhomie." He reacted to the sight of Americans warming the soles of their cowboy boots beside the fire while the vinyl of irreplaceable records warped on the mantel. Delaney and Bonnie were always raising their voices, often not in song. Whitlock and Radle checked out the rural bar at the edge of Clapton's estate. Jim Gordon and Rita Coolidge carried on their romantic intrigue. With a large stake in Clapton's financial well-being, Stigwood's observers accused Delaney and Bonnie of taking advantage of him. He reportedly paid for their transit to Europe, and an employee of the ever-watchful manager sniped that Bonnie descended on the star at one hotel during the tour "yelling, literally howling at him for bread."

Oblivious to any conflict of interest in his dual roles as flack and critic, Connally tore into the act in the *London Evening Standard:* "They say no amount of hype can sell a bad product and they're right. But a certain degree of subtle persuasion never hurt anyone, not least Americans Delaney and Bonnie and Friends, who together with Eric Clapton last night, made their first appearance of their British tour at the Albert Hall. Delaney and Bonnie are currently the most fashionable fad of the rock sophisticates. Mick Jagger, George Harrison, and Clapton himself have all remarked variously on their being the best band in the world and in this way the whole British popular music industry has come to regard them with some kind of awe." But despite all the negativity and rough start, English fans warmed to them. Clapton was correct about his drawing power, and George Harrison ventured out of his seclusion to join the band for 6 nights. This album was the Bramletts' biggest hit, rising to 29 on the *Billboard* chart.

On top of that star power, the Bramletts' band included guitarist Dave Mason. From Worcester, England, Mason started in the music business as a roadie for the Spencer Davis Group when Stevie Winwood was the singer. With Winwood, he had helped start the famed band Traffic. Mason was a rock star in his own right before he joined Delaney and Bonnie Bramletts' band. The group's album came out of the tour's last concert in Croydon. The band sent the crowd home with plenty of the guitar playing they paid to hear, but the emphasis was not on the furious solos associated with Cream, Blind Faith, and Traffic. Every song ran a brisk 4 or 5 minutes, and the guitarists offered good-natured shuffles and short riffs of the kind championed by the Band's Robbie Robertson.

On the concert album, an arrangement of a Bobby Whitlock song, "Where There's a Will, There's a Way," featured a Clapton piece that was almost delicate in its deference to a drum solo by Jim Gordon. The album featured a nice slide guitar piece by George Harrison on a road song, "Coming Home," with an arrangement and energy that rose above its lame lyrics, written by Bonnie and Clapton. (Harrison was not formally introduced at the show, and his accompaniment went uncredited because of his strained situation with the Beatles.) "We've never been treated like this in our lives," Delaney told the crowd, "and we appreciate it."

But for all the talent and sheer volume and the Bramletts' energy onstage, from the opening song, "Things Get Better," the lead guitarist was really the bass player, Carl Radle. Radle's thumping, well-paused notes laid the floor of the music and maintained the rhythm, along with Gordon's drums, and composed their own patient melodies, always just out front of Bonnie's soul screams, the interweaving lead and rhythm guitars, and the horn blasts of Bobby Keys and Jim Price. The bass player from Tulsa stole the show.

The Bramletts' live album was the first of six records, made over a 3-year period, that convey the sound of Derek and the Dominos, and ironically, in some ways it was a better and more accurate preview of *Layla* than Clapton's solo debut, which immediately followed.

Recorded in London and Los Angeles in November 1969 and January 1970, that record had too many voices, too many players, and too many producers, As a consequence, some of it measured up against Clapton's best music and some of it was just bad. Atlantic overruled Delaney Bramlett's suggestion of a title, *Eric Clapton Sings*, in favor of the ho-hum *Eric Clapton*. Bramlett was eager to produce the album, he provided his band as the session players, he claimed songwriting credit on most of the cuts, and his singing was all over the record. Leon Russell, a couple of members of Buddy Holly's old group, the Crickets, and Stephen Stills also appeared. There were 13 credited singers and musicians. The sound was a far cry from the trio of Cream; both Clapton fans and critics bellowed their disapproval. Often his guitar got buried in the mix, and why would anyone start off an Eric Clapton record with an instrumental duo of the horn players, Keys and Price? Even the song title, "Slunky," was off-putting.

Clapton was still so insecure about his voice that Bramlett sang the songs on an initial track and then the guitarist followed in a sort of karaoke sing-along. After the sessions, while Bramlett waited for Clapton to finish and send along one last track, Robert Stigwood grew impatient and told Atlantic to ship the master tapes to Clapton in England. The star admitted botching the mix, so Atlantic gave the salvage job to Tom Dowd, the engineer of the label's Cream records. In fairness to Bramlett, the album he coaxed out of Clapton in the two studios was not exactly the one packaged by the record company. And Bramlett's mix was the one that would have given the most prominence to Clapton's guitar.

Still, the album got much better after the first five cuts, and it ended with Bramlett and Clapton compositions that anticipated the vocal style and lovely guitar play of *Layla*. Bramlett brought "After Midnight," written by his pal J. J. Cale, to the record, and the song became one of Clapton's signature hits. Until Clapton took "After Midnight" to the Top 20 that fall, the reclusive Cale had never heard one of his own songs on the radio. Clapton knew Cale only as "one of those people from Tulsa"; their association has carried on ever since. Another durable attention-getter was "Blues Power," a song Clapton wrote with Leon Russell, after Bramlett introduced them. Ever since the solo debut, one of Clapton's performance favorites has been the jump-beat shuffle he arranged with Bramlett, "Bottle of Red Wine." But the cut that showed Clapton at his guitar-playing best was the closer. And it was the one in which he found that sweet spot that good singers know.

But Clapton meant for his guitar playing to sound different. For this album he changed from a Gibson Les Paul to a Sunburst Fender Stratocaster, which made his arcs of exploration more melodic and emotive. He and Bramlett threw out the lyrics they initially wrote for "She Rides" and transformed it into one of Clapton's most elegant and hypnotic pieces, "Let It Rain."

Some critics of *Eric Clapton* speculated that Leon Russell forced his theatrics on Clapton's tender psyche. Russell was in fact a very welcome piano player (Bobby Whitlock at that point played only the organ) and his speed, ear, and Jerry Lee Lewis–style flourishes supplemented Clapton's guitar beautifully in the climax of "Let It Rain." Clapton had an energetic chorus of backup singers, who included Delaney and Bonnie Bramlett, Stephen Stills, Rita Coolidge, and ex-Crickets Sonny Curtis and J. J. Allison, but on this closing piece he showed that he didn't need all that help, and his performance was not karaoke. Clapton the emerging tenor found a baritone soul mate in Whitlock, answering and echoing Clapton's cries for rain in exactly the style of the southerner's Memphis heroes, Sam and Dave. Their same technique would later drive their song "Anyday" and other classics of *Layla and Other Assorted Love Songs*, but in the meantime, with Bramlett's ample help, Clapton composed, played, and sang a 5-minute piece of music that was as good as anything he ever did with Cream.

———

After recording his solo album, Clapton played with the Bramletts on part their monthlong tour of North America. But his exercise in dodging the limelight proved to be just another of his phases, and he moved on, ever restless. Clapton went back to England, where an employee of Stigwood reported: "You could tell Eric's condition just by looking at him. His eyes were like marbles." The implication was that he was drugged out or exhausted. Any artist would have been tired; over a 4-month period, Clapton immersed himself in sessions of the Plastic Ono Band, King Curtis, the Crickets, Stephen Stills, Ringo Starr, Howlin' Wolf, Billy Preston, and Jesse Ed Davis. And, he maintained his love affairs with Alice Ormsby-Gore, Cathy James, and Paula Boyd—while longing to betray George Harrison and run away with Pattie. Whatever his intake of chemicals, no wonder he looked dazed and confused.

Considering its intensity, his friendship with Delaney Bramlett rather quickly cooled. (Publicly, at least, Clapton never spoke much about Bonnie.) The lasting creative and personal bonds he made were with the Bramletts' sidemen, not with the singer and his wife. Clapton knew he had been used to advance Delaney's ambitions, and he later said of his solo debut: "In a way it was a vehicle for Delaney's frustrations with himself. He may have been projecting himself on me a lot. And that came across a lot on the record. I don't mind it at all. I enjoyed it and learned a lot in the process. He was prepared to be my coach, and no one had ever offered that to me before. He was the first person to instill in me a sense of purpose. And he was very serious about it. He was a very religious person, saying things like, 'You've got a gift. If you don't use it, God will take it away.' It was quite frightening when I looked at it that way."

If Delaney Bramlett angled to make a great deal of cash from his collaborations with Clapton, he was sorely disappointed. A subsequent divorce settlement transferred a body of Delaney's songwriting rights to his ex-wife. Today, if you buy the remastered *Eric Clapton*, you will read that Bonnie Bramlett co-wrote 8 of the 11 cuts. The idea that such a thing actually occurred draws a guffaw from the first musician the Bramletts hired, Bobby Whitlock.

Following his time at Leon Russell's Plantation, Whitlock lived in a rented home in Hollywood with housemates who included Rita Coolidge. According to *Rolling Stone*, during that period Coolidge and Jim Gordon spent almost all their spare time together. There was a piano in the Hollywood rental house, and one day Whitlock heard Gordon and Coolidge working at length on an instrumental piece. They giggled about which of them was the worse piano player. That day they were plunking out the tune that, against Whitlock's wishes, would be the coda added to "Layla." "I told Rita that I'd testify to any jury in the world that I'd heard them writing that," he said after the composition became immensely valuable. "She didn't make a nickel off that song because she was intimidated by Robert Stigwood."

In March 1970, Joe Cocker was enjoying a vacation in Jamaica. The English soul singer's voice and spasmodic delivery in the movie *Woodstock* had made him a huge star in America (the twitches and jerks, it turned out, were just his manner of playing air guitar). Suddenly he was informed that if he didn't fulfill a contract for a tour of the States, the powerful unions that stood to benefit from its staging were capable of forcing the withdrawal of his work visa. Cocker had just sacked his band, and in a panic he called Leon Russell to help bail him out. Russell got on the phone and in a flash recruited 11 musicians and 10 backup singers. A number of them were pals from Tulsa—Carl Radle and the drummers Jim Keltner and Chuck Blackwell. The rock 'n' roll orchestra also included Dave Mason, Rita Coolidge, Jim Gordon, and the horn players Bobby Keys and Jim Price. They put in 4 straight 12-hour days of rehearsal. "This is great, we've pulled it out of the frying pan," said Russell's fellow producer and Shelter Records partner Denny Cordell, "but we can't have three drummers—any one of them will do."

But Russell kept them all, plus a conga player. Soon,

Cocker would release his album *Mad Dogs and Englishmen* (named for a 1932 Noël Coward song), which went gold in sales. Cocker had already caused a sensation with his appearance in the movie *Woodstock*, and the documentary from his forced road tour likewise proved to be one of the best rock movies ever filmed. But Russell also had a persona that the camera loved, with the top hat and cross necklace over a shirt that said "Holy Trinity," the girlish caress and flip of his shoulder-length graying hair, the drawling dry wit matched by a piercing cynic's stare. Russell demonstrated that he could play both piano and lead guitar. He meant to steal the show while saving Cocker's ass, and the scheme worked. Within 3 years, he would be the biggest concert draw in the world.

Over 8 weeks, they played 58 shows in 48 cities (or 46 in 58 days, in some accounts). Cocker didn't come away with a great deal of affection for Russell. He must have respected and appreciated Russell's organizational magic, but he didn't appreciate him brazenly stealing movie scenes and carrying on as if *he* were the band leader. Cocker's best performance in the documentary was his interpretation of the Beatles' statement of the period, "With a Little Help from My Friends." The camera cut back and forth between the sweat-drenched singer and the dashing metronome of a drummer, Jim Gordon. In one motel room scene, Radle was seen manicuring about 2 pounds of marijuana.

For the two future Dominos, the tour was a madcap ride and a hefty paycheck. They also got to leave their names on some first-rate live music. (A lot of it also demonstrated the states they were in.) Gordon disdained the groupies—his girlfriend was Rita Coolidge. Up until then, the muscular 24-year-old's experience with drugs had mostly been recreational dope smoking, but he went after the stronger drugs on that tour as if trying to win a track and field event. Keltner said that his friend Gordon persuaded him to drop acid before they played a concert in Seattle. Keltner got so lost during "Bird on the Wire" that he fell apart. Onstage, Gordon tried to talk him through it, but Keltner threw down his drumsticks and walked off crying. Gordon bulled ahead, never missing a beat. Gordon later said that the entourage was larger than the others realized. "I had a feeling I was being watched," he said, "but it was all in the background."

Russell probably figured that a 2-month loan of musicians wasn't going to harm any enduring act, but Russell had lured away five members of the Bramletts' band. "When they left," Bonnie later told *Rolling Stone*, "we were the last to know, and it broke our hearts." And Delaney and Bonnie were not an enduring act—the duo faltered in America after Clapton left, and they divorced in 1972.

Whitlock, the first one into the Bramletts' band, was the last one to leave. Made miserable by their fighting, he flew home to Memphis and sought advice from a Stax mentor, the rhythm guitarist and songwriter Steve Cropper. Whitlock told Cropper that he couldn't go back but he was broke—he didn't know what to do.

Cropper said, "Why don't you call Eric?"

"*Eric?*" Whitlock responded. "You mean Eric Clapton? Christ, we hung out together, had a good time. But it was just a couple of tours."

"Call Eric," said Cropper, nodding at his hunch. Then he gave Bobby enough money to buy a plane ticket to London.

6

ALL THINGS MUST PASS

BOBBY WHITLOCK ARRIVED at Eric Clapton's estate in the spring of 1970. He paid the cabbie and approached the portico, carrying a guitar case and a small bag of clothes.

"Bobby!" Clapton cried on seeing him. "What are you doing here?"

"But I called," Whitlock stammered. "I told you I was coming."

"Yeah, but I didn't think you'd *do* it."

Clapton later described Whitlock's voyage to Surrey as "an instinctive move." He made his recent bandmate feel welcome—there was plenty of room. The interior of the mansion was sparsely furnished. The sprawling living room had a sofa and a couple of chairs, its walls decorated only with a framed blowup of a photo in which a setter hiked a rear leg and pissed on a wall of corrugated metal marked by the graffiti "Clapton Is God." The straw mats and oriental rugs on the floors had the mustiness of a place whose owner loved the company of dogs. But the mansion was hardly empty. Whitlock remarked, "Eric kept everything, I mean *everything*, he ever owned. There were kids' clothes, old

T-shirts and caps, school reports and drawings, including one from 1958 labeled 'Eric Clapton, King of the Guitar.'" In the manor's taller wing, stairs wound past the master bedroom to a bare room with arched windows and a fireplace. This was the designated "music room," but Whitlock said all their playing went on downstairs, near the living room's fireplace. He arrived during an early spring that felt like winter. "It was a big rundown house with no heat," he said of Hurtwood Edge. "There was a fireplace and that was it, Jack. It was cold."

Guitars abounded. Some were collector's items, but Clapton was always tinkering with his instruments, taking off wang bars, making sure the action or give of the strings was exactly ⅛ inch throughout. He had found the guitar of his choice by associating sound with an image: "The LP cover of *Freddie King Sings the Blues*—he was playing a Les Paul! I went out after seeing that cover and scoured the guitar shops and found one. That was my guitar from then on, and it sounded like Freddie King." Except then he fell in love with the Fender Stratocaster: "When I get up there on stage, I often go through a great deal of indecision, even while I'm playing. If I've got the black Stratocaster on and I'm in the middle of a blues, I'm kind of going, 'Aw, I wish I had the Les Paul.' Then again, if I were playing the Les Paul, the sound would be great, but I'd be going, 'Man, I wish I had the Stratocaster neck.' I'm always caught in the middle between those two guitars. I've always liked the Freddie King/B. B. King rich tone; at the same time, I like the manic Buddy Guy/Otis Rush Strat tone. You can get somewhere in the middle, and that's usually what I end up doing, trying to find a happy medium. But it's bloody anguish." Clapton was like a hot rodder souping up and customizing a car. He built his most famous guitar, which he called Blackie, with parts of at least five guitars.

Clapton and Whitlock worked on tunes and lyrics daily, but at a measured pace. They were under no pressure to create anything. Clapton liked hearty English breakfasts—eggs and bacon and tea. They took the meals at truck stops, where he might be recognized as the guitarist of Cream, but there were no crushes of adulation and intrusion. Whitlock always paid his share.

The guitarist still kept a flat in London, though he had less privacy there and was wary of cops who were keen for drug busts of pop stars and the headlines they generated. One place or another, he kept up his romantic liaisons with Cathy James and with Alice Ormsby-Gore. That spring, however, Ormsby-Gore was on an extended holiday in Israel, which freed up Clapton's time for Paula Boyd.

Meanwhile, Whitlock was left to his own devices whenever his host was away. He turned 22 at Hurtwood Edge, but he would persist in remembering himself during that time as a teenager—perhaps because he behaved like one. "If anything happened, I was gonna be the one behind it," Whitlock recalled. "I'd reach out and knock over a glass, which would in turn knock over another one. That was me." He went for a ride on Clapton's motorbike and smashed it, bending the handlebars. Another occupant of the manor was Clapton's grandmother's parrot, Maurice. The bird was always calling, "Where's Eric? Where's Eric?" Whitlock loved birds—free birds, of course. Taking care not to get bitten, he lifted the parrot out its cage one day and set it on top of the wire enclosure. Then he couldn't resist giving it a poke. The parrot squawked, spread its wings, and glided straight into the ungrated fireplace. "Oh, no!" yelled Bobby. He ran across the room and snatched the bird from the flames and coals. Its feathers were singed and smoking.

Whitlock tidied up the parrot as best he could and put it back in its cage. Later he was compelled to report, "Eric, I let the bird out and he flew into the fireplace."

Clapton stared at him in amazement. "He's never been out of his cage his whole life, and you let him out?"

The star was miffed, but he didn't show Bobby the door. They kept getting ripped—mostly on grass, cocaine, and whiskey—and they played for hours. When Clapton wrote music, he always heard it first as a guitar piece. When it came together in his hands and instrument, then he could begin to think of words. Clapton and Whitlock had never worked together in this way before, but they found that they were a remarkable team of collaborators. "'Anyday' we just sat down and wrote," Whitlock said. "'Why Does Love Got to Be So Sad'—same thing. We started doing that intro on the bottom end of the guitar neck, then Eric whipped up to the top end and it started sounding right. Songs just evolved, like they did with Isaac Hayes and David Porter"—Whitlock's heroes from the Stax days in Memphis. "We weren't writing to have great songs; we wrote just to have something to play."

But Whitlock had come over with a few hundred bucks in his wallet. One day he had to blurt, "Eric, I've really enjoyed this. But I've got to go back. I have to work out something with an airline. I don't have a ticket."

With a look of astonishment Clapton replied, "Why are you going back?"

"Well, I think I have about £2."

"Why didn't you tell me you didn't have any money?"

"It never came up," said Bobby. "That's not why I'm here. I like hanging with you. Playing with you."

"What are you going to do when you get back?" Clapton asked.

"I don't know. Have no idea. I don't know what's going on in my life."

Clapton said with disappointment: "I thought we were starting a band."

———

And so it turned out the spring of 1970, they were. Clapton said after a moment, "I don't have any money either. Let's go see my manager." That day in London, Whitlock met Robert Stigwood, his future nemesis.

The bon vivant manager cut a striking figure—expensive suits, shoes as gleaming as his gab, a cigarette constantly in hand. When British rock stormed the earth in the mid-sixties, Stigwood went broke twice in the hustle. One of the Beatles' business representatives pegged him as "a real carnival promoter . . . a man who had 2 cents but could run up a bill."

The foundation of the Robert Stigwood Organization had been his recognition in 1966 of Cream's star potential. Stigwood's agency, expanded into a sublabel of Polydor, relied on his ability to roll those contracts over into Blind Faith and whatever else Clapton had a mind to do. In 1967, Stigwood incorporated an enterprise called Marshbrook Limited on Clapton's behalf, sheltering him from Britain's voracious tax system, and he aggressively managed his star's interests. But Stigwood had also managed to purchase a controlling interest in the Beatles' enterprise from manager

Brian Epstein without the band's knowing. According to biographer Bob Spitz, Stigwood and a partner moved the deal along by taking Epstein to Paris for a "dirty weekend" of chasing boy prostitutes. Beyond that, it's not clear what their personal relationship was. After Epstein collapsed and died in his flat in August 1967, the Beatles consented to a meeting with Stigwood, never having had the pleasure. He proceeded to tell them that he would be their new manager. John Lennon glared and said, "We don't know you. Why would we do this?" Stigwood walked away from the rebuff, though, with a nifty buyout of £26,000.

While still a partner of Epstein, Stigwood announced that he had fallen in love with a headshot photo of the Brothers Gibb, better known as the Bee Gees. Before they had sold a record, he pronounced them the next Beatles and launched them in America with a chartered cruise off Manhattan on a yacht full of celebrities. Stigwood personally rolled out the band that would become the progenitors of disco—and he did it on the Beatles' dime. Stigwood's impulse in response to the *faces* of the Bee Gees was characteristic. Clapton's manager was a flamboyant gay, and he was acquisitive.

When Clapton brought Whitlock to Stigwood's office, Bobby was slight and had unblemished features—the handsomeness of a young Tony Curtis, with a crown of curls like a Greek statue. "He took one look at me," Whitlock claimed, "and said, 'He's *mine.*'"

"No, he's not," Clapton intervened quickly. "We're putting a band together. We're going to play some rock 'n' roll."

"Great," the manager said, still grinning. "What do you fellows need?"

"We need some money. Get us a draw."

For several years that was how Clapton, and now Whitlock, went about living the good life as rock 'n' rollers in England. They went to Stigwood's office, they asked for cash, and they received.

Clapton set his partner up with the Hammond B-3 keyboard he favored and later bought him a Porsche so he could get about on his own. As they went on playing and writing, they talked about whom they wanted in the band. Their first choice, an easy one, was the bass player from Delaney & Bonnie and Friends. Carl Radle's personality was solid as a rock, they both liked him immensely, and he laid out a terrific blues bass line. Whitlock tracked down his friend, who had just staggered out of the wild finish of the *Mad Dogs and Englishmen* tour, his nerves jangled but his finances improved. Great experience, Radle reported, but it was insane. After the tour, Radle and Jim Gordon had gone back to Delaney Bramlett and said that they would like to have their jobs back, but they needed more money. Bramlett told them they were fired. Radle was thrilled at the prospect of joining a new band behind Clapton and said he would be over in a few days.

"The best drummers I've ever seen," Whitlock said, "were Jim Keltner and Jim Gordon. Fantastic players. Our first choice was Keltner. We called him and told him what we had in mind. He was all for it, but he had just gone in the studio to help make a jazz album. He'd said he'd be over the minute he was through. In the meantime, Carl had told Jim Gordon where he was going, and, man, Gordon was Johnny on the spot. He knew he wanted in on it, and he just presented himself, showed up on the doorstep with Carl. Eric and I talked about it. We were hot to get going. I said, 'Eric, they're both great drummers, but Keltner's tied up in the studio making that record. Gordon is *here*."

The first time Clapton had seen Jimi Hendrix, he had been awed at the way he could play rhythm and lead guitar at once. Clapton could manage that, but it required immense concentration, and he valued having a good second guitarist in the band. "Sometimes you end up playing every lick you know before the end of the set," he said of the continual solos in Cream, "and then you're fucked, you know, because you end up just repeating yourself over and over again." Clapton knew and respected Dave Mason, the ex of Traffic and the Bramletts' band. Mason was back in his native England now and, like the others, ready for new ventures. Mason had prospects for a solo album of his own, but despite the fact that he was seldom around during the germination of Clapton's new band, he agreed to play second lead.

Clapton and the three Americans set up their instruments in one of the large downstairs rooms. They jammed for hours, mastered old blues favorites, and honed their new material. Even with a 16-acre buffer, the commotion roused the neighbors; after a couple of protests, Clapton said they'd better tone it down. It wasn't just his consideration. He didn't want to give the authorities warrant to inspect the premises and deliver him in handcuffs to a feast for the tabloids. A year earlier—on Paul McCartney's and Linda Eastman's March wedding day, 1969—Pattie had called George Harrison in late afternoon and told him that police were ransacking their house in Esher in search of drugs. They found hash and weed. Wearing a yellow suit, according to the Beatles' biographer Robert Spitz, Harrison arrived in a stretch

89

limousine with his lawyer and exploded. Cops had their feet propped on the furniture, watching TV. One was looking at George's record collection. A photographer fired off a flash, igniting a scene worthy of a Beatles movie. Harrison chased the fleeing photographer, yelling that he was going to kill the guy, while the cops chased him. As he was pulled away by a friend, Harrison yelled at a reporter: "The fox has its lair; the bird has its nest. *This is my fucking house!*"

Hurtwood Edge was ripe for an uglier scene. Some accounts have speculated that Clapton was introduced to and pressured to take hard drugs by his comrades, especially Radle and Gordon. But Whitlock maintains that they all pitched headlong into drugs, and it was wholly voluntary. They were smoking a lot of opiated hash and tossing down Scotch. They got second, fourth, and sixth winds from cocaine. In those days, at least in that crowd of consumers, if you bought coke in Britain, you paid for and received an equal supply of heroin. Clapton and Whitlock both said the packets of junk piled up in a drawer.

"I was with Eric the night he first did heroin," Whitlock said. "He said it was the only one he hadn't done, and he kept going on about Robert Johnson, Ray Charles. You know— 'If I do it, then I'll get the blues.' I was saying, 'Man, you can write the blues in the back of a fucking limousine. You do not need heroin to write the blues. You do not need that experience.'"

Well, perhaps the Southerner did not advance that argument just then. "We were in the tea room," Whitlock described the occasion. "It was pink Chinese heroin. I didn't do it that night; I wanted to see what happened to him. I watched him do it and said, 'How does it feel?' He said, 'I feel like I've got cotton wool around me—warm and safe.'"

Clapton never got hooked on the needle. The heroin that came his way was pure enough—and he had sufficient money to buy it in quantity—that he could get what he needed snorting it like cocaine.

"So the next night," Whitlock said, "I went to the tea room, and I did it. My whole perception changed that instant. In a blinding flash everything in my life changed. For better or worse, I couldn't say. I didn't like it as much as Eric did. I hate throwing up. He tolerated it better, didn't get sick. But the time would come when I was locked up in a room in New York City, doubled up backward, calling for my mama. Heroin is addictive because it's the best drug in the world. It was something I had to go through. We all went through it. And there was a lot of it."

———

The day in January 1969 that George Harrison blew up at Paul McCartney over his arrogant lecture about guitar playing, it seemed that George might be the one to rupture the band. Lennon said blithely, "If he doesn't come back by Tuesday, we get Clapton. . . . We should go on as if nothing's happened." The following September, as Lennon summoned his nerve to actually do the deed, he decided to perform live for the first time in 3 years at a Toronto rock festival. Clapton had just returned to England from the long haul with Blind Faith and his stopover with the Bramletts in California, but when Lennon asked him to join the pickup Plastic Ono Band, he got back on the plane and ran through rehearsals at 30,000 feet. Exhilarated by being onstage again,

Lennon told Clapton on the way back that he wanted him to join his new band.

As provocative as that sounds—and Clapton was certainly under the artistic spell of Lennon—it is inconceivable that he would have done either of those things to George Harrison. Yet he obsessed day and night about running off with the man's wife.

Harrison had performed with Clapton's new band during Delaney and Bonnie and Friends' tour of England, and he probably came around to Hurtwood Edge and heard them working on the new material; in any case, he knew how good they were. Clapton described getting that phone call from Harrison: "We'd just got together and were rehearsing and living at my house, and we had no gigs, there was no game plan at all. We were just living there, getting stoned, and playing and semi-writing songs. When George said, 'Can I use some of the guys?' I said, 'Yeah, help yourself!'"

Quickly, though, Clapton's thoughts snapped to what might be in this for him. "Let's just make a deal," he proposed. "It'd be nice if we could get Phil Spector"—the Beatles' and now Harrison's producer—"to produce something for the band."

"Okay," said Harrison. "What we'll do is get Phil to produce an A- and B-side for you and then we'll use the band for my album."

They worked on *All Things Must Pass* at the Apple, Abbey Road, and Trident Studios from May through July of 1970. Harrison performed like a thoroughbred that had been given its head to run. A number of star musicians contributed to those sessions, among them Ringo Starr on drums, Billy Preston on organ, Klaus Voormann on bass, Dave Mason on lead guitar, Bobby Keys on tenor sax, Jim Price on trumpet, and Pete Drake on pedal steel. But in a 30th anniversary rerelease of his record, Harrison credited Eric Clapton, Bobby Whitlock, Carl Radle, and Jim Gordon as the indispensable core band.

The intimacy and long hours of the recording also gave Clapton a renewed chance to pursue what he had been dreaming about. Intoxicated by the attention he lavished on her, and angry with her husband for the lack of same, Pattie turned up the level of her flirtation with Eric.

Clapton was almost out of his mind for her. He drank to an astonishing extreme, and he ingested enough cocaine and heroin to put a spike through his heart. Whitlock, no angel himself, said he made a discreet and friendly observation to Clapton that he was too wasted to play well during one session. "I told Eric in Abbey Road that he was playing off-key. Not too quiet or loud—out of *tune*. He almost decked me."

One of the most intriguing aspects of those recording sessions is Jim Gordon's account of them. Gordon claimed that when the *Mad Dogs* tour ended, Harrison called and asked him to come to England to work on his solo album with Clapton and producer Phil Spector. In Whitlock's and Clapton's telling of the Dominos' origins, Gordon had effectively horned in, at the expense of his friend Jim Keltner. In Gordon's account, Clapton asked him to join his band after the Harrison sessions wrapped up. So he agreed and got himself a flat in Chelsea and a Ferrari. The band was an alliance of equals in Gordon's mind; he was not just a sideman. None of his fellow musicians had an inkling that anything but the drugs, booze, and wonder of their experience was affecting their drummer, but the voices that Gordon had heard since childhood were provoking him again—and one of their mutterings was that Clapton was a pretentious and arrogant prick who thought he was better than Gordon and was possibly out to get him, too.

In more startling and forbidding fashion, Gordon's romance with Rita Coolidge had recently come to an end. Coolidge said that she and other musicians in the *Mad Dogs* tour were in New York to play a concert, and they were staying at the Warwick Hotel. She said of Gordon, "He asked me to step out into the hall. I thought he wanted to talk; instead he hit me." Gordon knocked her down and blackened her eye; it stayed bruised for the rest of the tour. And they hadn't been arguing that she could recall. Gordon had bought her an expensive fur coat when they were dating, and now that he had decked her, he was deeply apologetic. He sent her books of poetry, but Coolidge was afraid of him and would have nothing more to do with him. Gordon was an ambitious and volatile young man, and he had a lot of things going on in his mind and career besides this pickup band in England. His ego conflict with Clapton was not yet transparent, but it was brewing, and it was angry.

Whitlock had never played the piano before they recorded the haunting "Beware of Darkness." Billy Preston wanted to play organ on that cut. The piano and organ of an electric keyboard look like the same instrument, but they are very different. Whitlock just plunged ahead, with a style of play in which he locked his wrists and stabbed at the keys from a distance of about 6 inches. Whitlock's play—along with that of Preston—delivered the bell-like tone characteristic of the

Beatles' albums. Harrison pulled off tricks and surprises in the manner of the old band, such as combining the familiar trumpet-led horns with the country-sounding pedal steel on the last chorus of "All Things Must Pass." Jim Gordon's short drum rolls, which sounded almost disco, were featured in "I Dig Love," which played with the theme of the period comedy *The Pink Panther.*

Clapton admired Harrison's ability to invent melodic lines on the scales, and as he had on "While My Guitar Gently Weeps," he came out of his rhythm accompaniment with some beautiful riffs and balancing melodies. The evolving direction of Clapton's band is obvious on two jams later included on the record—the Chuck Berry tribute "Thanks for the Pepperoni" and the intricate if laborious 11-minute "Out of the Blue." But with Carl Radle's thumping steadiness and sheer delight—he was the credited bass player on every song that made the finished album—the band's burgeoning sound also jumped out in "Wah-Wah," "Art of Dying," "What Is Life," "Let It Down," and the exquisitely phrased "Isn't It a Pity" and "My Sweet Lord." While Lennon, McCartney, and Starr floundered in search of their individual voices, Harrison surprised many by turning out one of rock 'n' roll's most durable achievements. His singing, playing, and arrangements were impeccable—that, and he had the luxury of Derek and the Dominos as his studio band.

7

REHEARSALS

Any man who could write "Something" understood the treasure of having Pattie for his lover and wife. Peter Brown, a Brian Epstein protégé and gossip who oversaw the Beatles' record stores, said of her: "Pattie always managed to look fabulous with very little effort." John Lennon's first wife, Cynthia, wrote in a memoir of the Beatle years, "Whenever fashions changed Patti [*sic*; though many, including Clapton, used the shortened spelling] was in there first with all the right gear looking as beautiful as ever." She opened her home to George's unending stream of friends, and at night when he arrived she had the dinner and wine planned, and the air was fragrant with freshly lighted incense.

Yet after just 4 years, this uncommonly fortunate marriage was wobbly. In Bob Spitz's biography of the Beatles, Brown gossiped about the four musicians' notorious philandering: "George was the worst runaround of the bunch. He had lots of girlfriends. Lots." Pattie's husband's infidelities, which were not always discreet, were just part of the humiliation. At first, Pattie embraced her husband's love of Asian culture, mysticism, and philosophy. The day that George announced their marriage, he said he'd been wondering what it would feel like to wake up inside Ravi Shankar's sitar. She accompanied George to Bombay to meet the virtuoso of Indian classical music, and their pilgrimage transformed Shankar into a pop icon in the West. (Without Harrison's boosterism, Shankar would have continued to be unknown to most British and American audiences, and he almost certainly would not have had the affair in New York in which he fathered the gifted jazz singer Norah Jones.)

Pattie's first experience with LSD left her cowering before the lights and noise of Leicester Square. George described his initial trip that same night as a "light bulb" of spirituality, though he later denounced LSD in strong terms after observing the squalid street "bums" of Haight-Ashbury. Pattie practiced Transcendental Meditation, and in a scene described by Spitz, she was among those gathered around the Maharishi Mahesh Yogi in the Beatles' first audience: In a compartment of a train speeding away from London, the Maharishi received them while seated lotuslike on a mat and cushion of flowers. After a subsequent audience with the Maharishi, George explained that they "were looking to establish that which was within." Ren Grevatt, an American critic for the British publication *Melody Maker*, wrote drily: "I've noticed that George Harrison is getting deeper and deeper every day and will probably end up being a bald recluse monk. He's trying to figure out life, but don't let this sound mocking—he's very serious."

The "youngest Beatle," as Harrison was continually called, was 27 years old when the band broke up. It was time for George to grow up—and, in Pattie's view, to stop taking their marriage for granted. He was loved by one of the most desirable women on earth, but he kept driving them further apart. Pattie was not happy about being ignored, and she had this sexy young guitar player constantly around who was madly in love with her. In secluded encounters, she'd go right to the brink of making love to Eric and then pull back, which left all their nerve endings jangling and aroused. Pattie was indulging this and letting it continue, she later admitted, so she could make her husband jealous. She was playing with emotional fire.

Clapton not only obsessed about going to bed with her—he wanted to possess her, run away with her. His view of his unrequited love took on the anguish of a martyr. In his Clapton biography *Crossroads*, Michael Schumacher wrote that the star's state of mind in early 1970 lurched between "depression, loneliness, despair, confusion, sadness, and frustration." And anger. He was angry that George's quest for religion was making Pattie so unhappy. It made him hostile toward all religion, including the born-again Christianity he had professed.

With emotional torment of her own, Pattie continued to see him and hold him off sexually. She was manipulating and punishing Clapton, but at the same time she was trying to be good—to remain faithful to her husband and her marriage vows. Harrison was so preoccupied with his record album and inner voyage that he seemed oblivious to the intrigue of seduction and possible cuckoldry.

Alice Ormsby-Gore was still away on her long holiday in the Middle East—so he didn't have to mask his overpowering attraction to George's wife. Pattie's sister Paula enjoyed a period of his company and pursuit; she was hopeful that Clapton cared for her. He used Paula Boyd in much the same way Pattie used him. As always, he channeled his emotional life into his music. With a gift for compartmentalizing that was almost scary, Clapton poured his heart into helping Harrison make a brilliant and enduring album—all the while angling for the chance to betray their friendship. Given Clapton's long conversations with Pattie and his conclusion that George was making her life miserable with his incessant spirituality, he must have played rhythm chords to George's slide lead on a future number one hit, "My Sweet Lord," with a certain sense of irony.

Billy Myles was a singer and songwriter who enjoyed a burst of hit singles in the doo-wop period, peaking with "The Joker (That's What They Call Me)." During the time that Myles's peers and stablemates on the same label, the Silhouettes, stormed Top 40 radio with the teen trifle "Get a Job," the quasi-soul singer wrote "Have You Ever Loved a Woman," later covered by Clapton's idol Freddie King. Clapton had played guitar in performance of Myles's piece since his days with John Mayall's Bluesbreakers, but his own singing and arrangement transformed and claimed it as his personal blues, making it into a cry of love and pain for a best friend's wife. But in contrast to the lyrics, Clapton was unlikely to make a moral decision that his love was not sufficient reason to break up the Harrisons' marriage and home. Between Clapton's endless knowledge of rhythm and blues poetry and the new songs he was writing with Whitlock, he was well on his way to telling the story that was eating him alive.

Crazy with a love that so far had given him mostly grief,

Clapton had read a book of poetry called *Khamsah of Nizami*. The Bedouin legend of Majnun and Layla and the book of 12th-century Persian verse were fairly well known in Britain. A Worcestershire sauce tycoon had obtained a lavishly illustrated copy of the book commissioned by a Mogul emperor in the 16th century; in 1958, the tycoon passed it on to the British Museum, and in turn the British Library commissioned a translation of the book and kept it in print. In future years, Clapton would shrug on some occasions and say he just thought "Layla" was a pretty name. He said, "I had no idea what 'Layla' was going to be. It was just a ditty." But Clapton's projection of himself into Nizami's narrative and verse utterly belied his nonchalance.

Clapton had a fine ear for the poetry and anecdotes of his blues heroes, from the killer and convict Leadbelly to Robert Johnson, who sang boastfully of walking side by side with Satan. Clapton was also known to quote English poets from the late 18th and early 19th centuries—Samuel Taylor Coleridge, William Blake. He may not have read widely, but he understood the power of language and story. And in 1970 it was hardly surprising that a young Briton with a bad case of unrequited love would read and project himself into the legend of Majnun and Layla. The record forming in Clapton's mind might have been termed a concept album by a more detached artist, but this was no representational gift to Pattie. Clapton *believed* he was going mad.

———

The Americans in Clapton's band couldn't help knowing about his brokenhearted love and lust for George's wife. They neither passed judgment nor tried to help move the affair to fruition. There was a certain bar where Eric and Pattie felt they could meet and talk discreetly, and when Clapton's bandmates saw them there, they left them alone.

But the players shared Clapton's artistic vision instinctively and completely. In the endless jams at Hurtwood Edge and in the studio sessions behind George Harrison, they helped Eric coax his dream into being. When they were playing music, his passion was their passion.

With the release of Clapton's solo debut album and the radio-targeted single, J. J. Cale's "After Midnight," set for August 1970, Robert Stigwood was nervous about signals that the sales response would be weak. On behalf of Clapton's corporate entity, Marshbrook Limited, and his own enterprise, Stigwood always favored promotional extravaganzas on the order of Cream and Blind Faith. But that was the last thing Clapton wanted. In search of a more melodic and emotive sound, he bought six different Fender Stratocasters from a favorite dealer that summer. The new band wasn't going to sound like Cream, and they weren't going to go out before they were ready and embarrass themselves, like Blind Faith. Clapton had said before the latter tour began, "If only Blind Faith could go out to a club in Haslemere or somewhere and go on as the Falcons, it would take all the pressure off us."

An ally in Clapton's cautious strategy, Roger Forrester was an emerging force in the star's life. A police constable's son who had got his start as a booking agent, Forrester was skillfully maneuvering within the Robert Stigwood Organization to become Clapton's sole manager. With so much riding on Clapton's emergence as a solo star and singer, Forrester wanted no jarring headlines or controversial interviews.

Clapton and Forrester made a plan in which the band would hone the new material in small clubs and ballrooms across England. Clapton wanted knowledge of them to spread by word of mouth, with minimal advertising, and in a nod to the masses, every ticket would cost just £1.

"He *becomes* different people," Clapton's publicist observed to a writer for the *Sunday Times*. "When he was with [Harrison] he bought a big house like George's and a big Mercedes. . . . When he met Delaney and Bonnie he gave up traveling first class and just climbed onto their bus." Whoever Clapton was now, the mascara, flowing scarves, and skintight silk pants were long gone; the new look was jeans, boots, and ordinary long-sleeved shirts. In a small gesture of defiance of authority, dangling from a thin necklace was his coke and heroin spoon. His brown, unpermed hair just reached his jaw and collar, and he was in one of his clean-shaven periods—once more recognizable as a village lad. Thin in the chest and arms, he looked as if he had missed too many meals. Still, admirers straight and gay noted that the boots and jeans showed off sexy legs. At 25, he was quite a handsome man.

Clapton, his American houseguests, and Dave Mason wound up their work on Harrison's album and began the band's trial run at London's Lyceum Ballroom on June 14, 1970. The Lyceum was a chic venue; Clapton had performed there the preceding December with John Lennon and the Plastic Ono Band, and the bill for this concert read "Eric Clapton and Friends." They wouldn't have to worry about empty chairs or drunks talking loudly through the songs. As they waited to go out and begin, the talk turned to the earnest but comic ritual of naming the band. Tony Ashton, an

LAYLA AND OTHER ASSORTED LOVE SONGS BY DEREK AND THE DOMINOS old friend of Clapton's, was backstage; Ashton always called Clapton by the nickname Del, and he threw out the suggestion of Del and the Dominos: perhaps in tribute to the great Fats Domino, or a rhythm-and-gospel outfit from the early fifties named the Dominoes (fronted first by Clyde McPhatter and then Jackie Wilson), or perhaps apropos of nothing at all. In a few minutes Del evolved into Derek, which suggested a dashing alter ego for Eric. "We didn't have a name up to that point," Clapton recalled. "You don't think of that when you're forming a group. In fact, when someone suggests to you that you get a band title, that's when you really start to worry about whether you should have a band at all, because you realize so much hinges on the name and you've blown the whole gig no matter what the music's like.

"It wasn't a conscious attempt at anonymity," Clapton went on. "We presumed that everyone would know what it was all about. That it would be an open joke." The house announcer heard it wrong and introduced them as Derek and the Dynamos.

The Lyceum was the only gig in which Dave Mason actually played second lead in the new band. He helped them record one side of their single, but his solo opportunity compelled him to quit the band and leave abruptly for his own promotional tour. At the Lyceum they held the set to nine numbers, with Clapton performing songs from his solo album and offering his fans one favorite from the Cream days, "Crossroads." He played intently and made a brave show, with the help of Whitlock and Mason, of singing with confidence. The finale was a new song written by Clapton and Whitlock, "Tell the Truth." It had no connection to a rhythm and blues hit of that title recorded in the fifties by Lowman Pauling's Five Royales, Otis Redding, and most energetically, Ray Charles. However, the song and its arrangement did employ the call-and-response routine that Whitlock so admired in his Memphis rhythm and blues upbringing, while watching Sam and Dave.

"'Tell the Truth' I wrote one night after we'd been up for days on one of our marathons," Whitlock said of the jams at Hurtwood Edge. "We used to just play and play and play. We would literally play for 3 days without stopping. Anyway, I was up by myself sitting in Eric's living room when this thing just hit me. . . . I was a young man, gaining experience and getting older; that's what I was thinking about." He made up the guitar chords on an open tuning he had learned from Duane Allman one time when Duane was hanging out with Delaney Bramlett. Whitlock played and sang his piece for Clapton, and they finished it together. The young man in the song thought he was so cool, but he was letting everything that mattered slip from his grasp.

A critic for a British music magazine yawned in his review of the Lyceum concert: "Ordinary—Eric in fairly dull debut." Another reviewer differed: "Eric leads and sings his heart out." But the most ardent critiques came from fans and concertgoers who were motivated enough to write letters. A correspondent to *Melody Maker* described leaving the Lyceum "feeling bored, bewildered, and thoroughly sick. Sick of people who cheer the name and not the music." In the most hostile biography of Clapton, *Edge of Darkness*, Christopher Sandford sampled scathing letters written about Clapton and his new band:

"Unless Eric Clapton finds his feet again as a good, fast and tasteful guitar player, the critics will find another."

"If Clapton wants to lose his crown to another young guitarist, he only has to carry on what he's doing."

Another disgruntled fan claimed to have been nauseated by the Dominos' show: "After seeing Clapton looking like a degreased Elvis Presley and playing poorly disguised rock and roll, I came away sick."

Four days after the Lyceum show, the band met Phil Spector and George Harrison at Apple Studios in London to fulfill the deal Eric had made with George. Their purpose was to record two tracks for a single release that would command airplay and, they hoped, whet the public appetite for an album. Dave Mason played on the projected B-side, "Roll It Over," but on the A-side the musicians were Clapton, Harrison, Whitlock, Radle, and Gordon. Their song, "Tell the Truth," was full of self-reproach, and for it to work, they would have to cultivate that cutting doubt. The version they recorded didn't quite work; the problem wasn't Spector's fabled "wall of sound" engineering control—rather, it sounded as if they sang and played the tune about 20 percent too fast. In Spector's production, the lyrics and the voices of Clapton and Whitlock flew by in meaningless garble: the song lost its insight and sense of humor.

Pumped up nonetheless, the Dominos settled back in Hurtwood Edge and continued writing and adapting new songs. That July Clapton, Whitlock, Radle, and Gordon played with Dr. John and a large supporting cast that included Mick Jagger and the Memphis Horns on an album, *Sun Moon and Herbs*, that was never released. And, sometime during those weeks, Eric finally made love to Pattie.

During the summer of 1970, she gave into her own frustration, temptation, and desire. There were assignations at Hurtwood Edge and in London. The biggest cultural event in London that July was the premiere of the play *Oh! Calcutta!* Offered as an "experiment in elegant erotica" by the playwright and critic Kenneth Tynan, the revue confronted the mores of London and the police department's obscene publications squad. The chic playwright of the contemporary American West, Sam Shepard, wrote one of the scenes; John Lennon contrived another about a masturbation club. Told to be prepared to make arrests for pornography, the undercover cops sat through a string of skits that were memorable only for the displays of nudity. No charges were filed, and the play ran for years.

Robert Stigwood hosted one of his galas after the play. George Harrison skipped the performance and worked late at the studio on *All Things Must Pass,* before heading to Stigwood's fete. Harrison, his Beatles mate Lennon would reflect, was "an intelligent man, who was thinking all the time; and all the time he was thinking that his best friend was sleeping with his missus." The revelation that this had occurred began when he pulled up and parked in Stigwood's drive that night. Eric and Pattie sashayed out right in front of him, arm in arm and laughing in a way that only a fool could deny.

———

Pattie Boyd knew the force of emotions that she and Clapton had just let out of the bottle. Clapton kept telling her that she had to leave her husband and run away with him. She asked herself what she was doing, then made love to him again

———

before telling him he was out of his mind; she was not about to leave George. When he was feeling strong and determined, Clapton told himself that he had to prove to her that they couldn't live without each other. When he was feeling weak, he despaired that it could never be.

What did the Dominos think of all this? It was easier for them once Harrison's album was finished. Through it all, Clapton maintained an eerie focus on his music. In August he and the Dominos resumed the tour of small clubs. They sped off in his Mercedes for some gigs, jumping on trains for others. In Hanley, Newcastle, Birmingham, Bournemouth, Malvern, Plymouth, they appeared loose and happy. Carl Radle and Clapton had become good friends when both were in Blind Faith; Radle was someone Eric could confide in. Radle said that tour of the clubs was "the moment Clapton rediscovered himself." Whitlock added, "Eric's playing began to come more from the heart than the wrist." But the Americans were thrilled not just with the big name in the band, but also with each other and the tour itself. They could gauge the reaction in the faces of people who writhed and bobbed at a distance of 5 feet. "When you play a small club tour of England," Whitlock laughed, "they are *small*. People were jam-packed right up to the stage. Carl wore those wire-rimmed glasses. One time I looked around and the body heat was so intense that his glasses were all steamed over.

"Another place, the backstage area was up some stairs. We were up there taking a break when this guy starts banging on a window. 'Hey, can I come in?' Well, we guess so! We hauled him through the window, gave him some whiskey. Here, blow a little smoke. I said, 'How the hell did you get up here?' We looked out the window, and all these guys had built a pyramid in the alley. They were standing on each others' shoulders, and he was the one who made it to the top."

One of the largest places they played was the Roundhouse in Nottingham. "It was a circular room with nine bars and us right out in the middle. We were playing 'Let It Rain' when a fight broke out between a longhaired guy and a skinhead. The more we played, the more they fought. It would start to die down, and then crank back up. We had that whole place in an uproar. It was revved-up garage band rock 'n' roll."

It wasn't like Cream, as many fans and critics complained, but Clapton was rocking, whether people liked it or not. The band crossed the Channel to France and rode down to Provence for a gig that failed to materialize. They stayed in the house of a friend named Emile de Schonberg, and in hedonistic rampage wrecked the place, especially a piano, resulting in apologies that went on for years. Their host's father, Frandsen de Schonberg, was an artist of distinction, and in that house Clapton saw the painting of an exotic and beautiful young blonde with evasive eyes and teardrop cheeks. It was uncanny how much the artist's image resembled Pattie. Clapton saw the painting and decided it had to be the cover art for the Derek and the Dominos' album.

His obsession with her didn't mean, though, that he had lost his eye and yearning for hundreds of women. During the foray into France they encountered "the Persian princess." Whether she was from Iraq, Iran, Jordan, no one seemed to know exactly—if the musicians were even acquainted with such nations. The girl spoke a language they could bridge only with the aid of a translator in her entourage. All the Americans knew about her was that she was beautiful, she was a member of some royal family in the Middle East, and for one week their leader fell in love with her. "She wore bell bottoms, and she was all hung up on Eric," said Whitlock. "She didn't speak a word of English and they had to date through an interpreter who was always with her. I never figured out how that worked. What do they do with him when it's time to take their clothes off?"

The princess, whoever she was and wherever she came from, was the inspiration of a new song they added to the repertoire. They started "Bell Bottom Blues" while they were still in France and finished it at Hurtwood Edge. Compared with the much-publicized squabbling of Lennon and McCartney, Clapton and Whitlock were a serene team of songwriters. Whitlock's only real complaint about his collaborator and very generous benefactor was that Clapton claimed sole credit for the song. Whitlock would sing the lines about the tormented lover offering to crawl on his knees for another chance, the humiliation of a man being forced to beg.

And then he'd giggle and jeer. "That's straight out of Stax Records, man! Albert King and Otis Redding. That ain't no upper-class *Englishman* talking."

Whitlock's taunt and intimation that he had a more legitimate claim to soul was unfair and inaccurate, of course. Though Clapton was fascinated by the airs and privilege of English nobility, he was born of villagers and construction tradesmen, and he was as dedicated to the nitty-gritty and the mythos of black American bluesmen as a white war baby could be; he just didn't have the luck and opportunity to hang on his heroes' every word and move in Memphis. In any case, Derek and the Dominos had no royalties to squabble over—yet.

REHEARSALS

8

MIAMI

TOM DOWD SAID HE LEARNED to hear music by working with Ray Charles and other blind artists. He meant that its structure and nuance come clearer to people who are not distracted by sight, and some, like Charles, were able to articulate that. Dowd was at the vanguard of an ongoing revolution in recording technology, but he arrived in the mixing booth almost by accident. His story, wonderfully told in the film *Tom Dowd and the Language of Music,* by Mark Moorman, began in Manhattan during the years between the World Wars. Dowd's father was a stage manager on Broadway, his mother a Sorbonne-trained operatic soprano. Dowd took up tuba for his public school band and learned to play the string bass, which helped him gain an appreciation of the bass line that builds the foundation of all recorded music. Tall and gangly, he was recruited out of New York City's prestigious Stuyvesant High School for the band at Columbia when he was 16. Before long he was the drum major at the halftime of football games. His field of study, though, was nuclear physics.

After the attack on Pearl Harbor, the government organized the Office of Scientific Research and Development, which sought to enlist the country's top academics and laboratories into the war effort. Dowd was assigned to work under a contract won by Columbia. Drafted into the army at 17, he went through boot camp in Louisiana, then was ordered right back to Columbia, officially assigned to the U.S. Army Corps of Engineers, Manhattan District—the district that gave its name to the Manhattan Project.

Dowd did not learn until near the end of the war that his team's research in nuclear spectrography—identifying and mapping the dispersion of radiation—was part of America's race to build an atomic weapon. Dowd assumed that he would go back to Columbia, complete his degree in about a year, and pursue a career as a nuclear physicist. However, he then found out that much of what he'd done during the war was classified—erased from his academic record—and if he began his study of physics all over again, he would be obliged to accept as fact scientific theories that the Manhattan Project's research had helped disprove. Just like that, Dowd was on the street, a guy with (it appeared) little more than a high school education.

From the frequency of sound waves and pitch to the 12 tones in an octave, technical understanding of music is rooted in mathematics, and so, bolstered by his scientific acumen, Dowd returned to music, his first love. Dowd nosed around New York recording studios and in 1947 scored a summer job in a control room where one day a woman named Eileen Barton sang an odd, folksy demo called "If I Knew You Were Comin' I'd've Baked a Cake."

The song became a hit, and it got Dowd's foot in the door, freelancing as a sound engineer. While Dowd had been testing theorems of radiation, Ahmet Ertegun, a son of a Turkish ambassador to the United States, had started a New York label called Atlantic Records. His partners included Jerry Wexler, a reviewer and critic for *Billboard*—he was the one who came up with the idea of scrapping the demeaning term *race records* (the common descriptor for music performed by African Americans) and invented a more inclusive catch-all: rhythm and blues. The Atlantic partners took a chance on Dowd—still just a gangly kid—one day when they were told that an imperious man they'd worked with a few times at another studio was busy engineering a record for the rival Mercury Records. By 1954 they had engaged Dowd to work exclusively for Atlantic; for a long time, he was the only engineer they used.

Ertegun and Wexler loved records that were popular with black audiences in the South and in cities such as Chicago. They staked their first claim to rhythm and blues with Stick McGhee's "Drinkin' Wine Spo-Dee-O-Dee," and for $3,000 they bought the contract of Ray Charles, who had been scraping by trying to sound like Nat King Cole. His first records for Atlantic, which attached racy lyrics to well-known gospel melodies, provoked some outraged sermons— a bit of sexy scandal is always a plus in the music business. Suddenly Atlantic was signing the Coasters, the Drifters, Ben E. King, Solomon Burke, LaVerne Baker.

Atlantic moved into jazz the same way it had with rhythm and blues. The company's engineering wunderkind found himself looking out from the controls and shepherding the sounds of Herbie Mann, Charlie Parker, Charlie Mingus, John Coltrane, and the Modern Jazz Quartet. When Dowd started out, a recording engineer was usually a moonlighting disc jockey. A needle of industrial diamond carved the sound directly to a vinyl master disc, 88 lines to an inch for a 2-minute song. Most LPs were recorded in a day. Dowd, though, transformed the engineering from single-track recording to stereo, he pioneered the use of ¼-inch tape instead of vinyl, and he delicately adjusted sound with eight-tracks a full 10 years before the celebrated producers of the Beatles and the Stax label's rhythm and blues stars knew that it was possible—they still thought three-tracks were state of the art. Dowd engineered Otis Redding's *Otis Blue,* and Atlantic assigned him to be Redding's emissary when he stormed Europe in triumph in 1966. When a 1967 session at Muscle Shoals for the newly signed Aretha Franklin collapsed after just 2 days—amid whiskey-fueled insults, one full-blown fistfight, and reports that a sideman tried to put the make on the 25-year-old star—Dowd raced back to New York with Franklin and Wexler and helped rescue *I Never Loved a Man the Way I Love You.*

Wexler cooled on recording in Memphis and Muscle Shoals after that incident and the plane crash that claimed Redding's life. Dowd was an inveterate New Yorker, but he was developing health problems aggravated by cold, wet winters, and in 1969 he jumped at the chance to move his family and head up a new Atlantic South operation in Miami. Criteria Recording, he said, was as well equipped as any studio in New York.

Dowd was an acquiring producer now, in addition to being a very opinionated engineer. He would get out on the studio floor with musicians, telling them to adjust this note or that measure. In August 1970 the Allman Brothers Band were glad to be in Miami recording their second album, *Idlewild South*, for an industry legend such as Dowd. That said, they were road-hardened, unabashed crackers, and Gregg and Duane were still smarting from the Hour Glass experience at the hands of record producers in California. Dowd was 20 years older than most of the guys in the Allman Brothers and their entourage, and they pegged him as someone whose musical tastes were shaped by the forties and big band jazz.

Dowd bridged his gaps with the suspicious Southern rockers because he loved and could follow their almost free-form compositions. He also had a distinct advantage coming in, because Duane Allman was the band's leader, and Dowd had been there when Wexler gave him all the Atlantic session work that began in Muscle Shoals. Like everyone at Atlantic, Dowd was crazy about the drawling and brilliant player.

Dowd disliked having his sessions interrupted by the telephone but one August day he was compelled to make an exception for Robert Stigwood, calling from London. Clapton's powerful manager said, "Eric has put a new band together and he'd like to record, and he's wondering if you have time...."

Dowd said, "Sure, we'll work it out."

Duane Allman walked into the control room with a guitar slung across his shoulder. Dowd apologized for having to take the call, then said, "Hey, that's a hot one, kid. That was Eric Clapton's management talking about him coming here to record."

Allman said, "You mean the guy from Cream?" At once he started playing Dowd some of Clapton's licks. "Man, are you going to record him? Oh, man, yeah, I gotta meet him. Do you think I could watch?"

***

At the beginning of the Mark Moorman documentary film about Tom Dowd, a middle-aged Clapton said of Dowd, "To be perfectly frank, I wasn't interested in people like that." He meant, looking back, that he was a young, egotistical know-it-all who thought that recording technicians were squares, albeit ones with essential expertise. Clapton eventually came to value Dowd as a wise friend for more than just his genius in the studio. He did respect Dowd's engineering of Cream's *Disraeli Gears* and *Wheels of Fire*, he was indebted for many favors in studio sessions, and he was grateful for Dowd's salvaging the mix of his solo album, which debuted just days before he flew into Miami with the new band. But Clapton was a man on a crusade of love and art, and in his young man's estimate of the universe, Tom Dowd was the help. Their relationship was cordial, professional, but not chummy.

"I had alerted the staff at Criteria that this was going to be brutal," Dowd said. "Bring earmuffs. Because these guys would be showing up with double stacks of Marshalls and God knows what." He would never forget the sight of Cream's roadies rolling into Atlantic's cramped studio with enough amplifiers to rattle Yankee Stadium's bleachers from home plate. Clapton's and Jack Bruce's guitars had been so loud that he had had a devil of a time placing a mike that would pick up Ginger Baker's drums. But when Clapton appeared this time, he strolled in with a Fender Champ and a battery-operated Pignose. Carl Radle had a piggyback Ampeg B15. Dowd said, "And I'm thinking, '*Whoaaaaaah*, what the hell is going on here?'"

Clapton's turn toward smaller amps was motivated in part by self-preservation. "I don't think I'll ever be the same," he said in a *Guitar Player* interview after Cream disbanded. "I think one ear is stronger than the other. One ear is at least half deaf; I don't know which one. When I'm onstage I have to stand a certain way to be able to hear everything." But the 25-year-old had also flummoxed a sound wizard with his knowledge and mastery of technology that was then unknown to Dowd. It was as if he were 10 years ahead in knowledge of the Beatles' engineers at Apple Studios. They recorded *Layla* with amplifiers that were about the size of a box of cereal.

The Leslie speaker hooked to Bobby Whitlock's Hammond B3 organ was put in the sound room, and the studio contained a grand piano shrouded by a boat-shaped canopy, to better contain its ring. At a slight remove from the others, Gordon set up his drums in an open carousel that could be revolved to best direct his playing to the mikes. The guitarists' tiny amps were set up on camp chairs. "If anybody walked into that studio with squeaky shoes, we'd blow a take," Dowd said. "That's how quiet they were. They weren't wearing earphones, so everybody could hear each other. Jim Gordon could hear everything that everyone else was playing in the room."

Dowd was always juggling projects. Despite his admiration for Clapton's past work as a musician and this demonstration of technical knowledge, Dowd was managing an assembly line of band and records; a session couldn't meander, and in his estimate, Clapton and his players had not come to his house well prepared. Whitlock seemed the primary author of a few songs they were proud of, but Clapton initially kept his work on "Layla" close to his vest; he seemed most intent on mining his treasured lode of old blues riffs and rhymes. In Dowd's view, they had some good ideas but not finished material.

Clapton and the players believed they were right on track. "We were very fit," Clapton said. "We would have saunas, go swimming during the day, and then go to the studio and get loaded. It didn't affect the playing or the sessions. But as is the way with drugs, it would catch up later." They tore into the songs, albeit quietly, just as they had at Hurtwood Edge, and kept at it for hours. They left large bags of heroin and cocaine lying around. They swigged like roughnecks from quarts of whiskey. One girlfriend came over from England to watch: Paula Boyd. She had been living at the manor with Clapton, but there had to be some cold rebuff; with his mind on her older sister, the relationship must have suffered. During the Miami sojourn, she took up with Whitlock and became his girlfriend.

Dowd was no innocent. He had engineered records by mainline junkies, people who left sessions to shoot up. But it was hard to believe that Derek and the Dominos' recklessness was going to improve their product or their prospects for long-term health. Dowd resolved to have some discreet words with Clapton. As the engineer did with disciplined jazz musicians, he listened to their starts on the material and expertly translated them to charts.

Common practice in recording studios, charts are not the formal scores used by symphonic musicians, but they are specific about who plays what and when. Since Dowd had no advance knowledge of these rock songs, he drew up the charts from listening to preliminary run-throughs. He walked through the studio handing the youths pieces of cardboard with written outlines for the parts they would be playing. That led to their first come-to-Jesus conversation. "What the hell is this?" Whitlock griped to Clapton. "Nobody has to tell us how to play this music. We've been working out these songs in your house. We rehearse on the road. That's what we do. We're a rock 'n' roll band."

Clapton agreed with him. The rebellious youths descended on Dowd with a variation on the famous line from *The Treasure of the Sierra Madre*. "Charts? We don't need no *steenking* charts." They made their point without acrimony, but Dowd was informed that his place was on the other side of the control room glass. Dowd's role was redefined and limited to executive producer. After Dowd's tacit demotion, the band composed and reshaped as they played.

This exertion of Clapton's power had an additional effect on the way in which the musicians went about their business. Dowd did advise the star that it might be wise if he and the guys toned down their recreational high jinks, and later Dowd maintained, perhaps because he was still employed by Atlantic Records, that Bobby Whitlock in particular exaggerated the drug use in the company's Miami studio. On hearing that, Whitlock laughed out loud. "If Tom had had any idea what we were doing in there, he would have shut that session down in an *instant*."

When Clapton and Dave Mason had agreed that Mason would not be the Dominos' second guitarist after all, Clap-

118

ton decided to go it alone. After all the concerts and recording sessions with Cream and Bad Faith, it wasn't as if he didn't know how to play without a rhythm guitarist backing him up. As it turned out, the parting was fortuitous for both parties. Mason was gifted, but *Layla* would have been a very different album if he had come to Miami.

In that period, Clapton broke his own style of play down into two fundamentals: "When I pick, I rest the butt or palm of my hand on the bridge of the guitar and use it as a hinge or lever. When I stretch strings I hook my thumb around the neck of the guitar. A lot of guitarists stretch strings with just their hands free. The only way I can do it is if I have my whole hand around the neck, actually gripping onto it with my thumb; that somehow gives me more of a rocking action with my hand and wrist." He played the guitar in a combination of up strokes and down strokes; he was amazed by jazz guitarists who in a blur could go up and down at once in a technique he called double-picking. He liked to think he knew his limitations, and initially there was no thought of bottleneck guitar being part of *Layla*'s sound.

Clapton loved George Harrison's serene way of playing slide and had enjoyed accompanying his friend on "While My Guitar Gently Weeps" and on several cuts of *All Things Must Pass*. On occasion, Clapton played some bottleneck on his acoustic guitar, but he never attempted it onstage or in the studio. Also, despite the prominence of bottleneck guitarists in the blues pantheon, he thought that many of the riffs had grown formulaic and hackneyed, and he had been wounded by Jon Landau's broadside in *Rolling Stone* that he was the master of blues clichés. He didn't want to be accused of appropriating another.

In the serendipity that often changes and improves art, slide guitar became part of the composing and arrangement when Tom Dowd got a call from Duane Allman that his band was back in Miami to play a benefit concert. On August 26th and 27th, the recording engineers and the band "fumbled along," as Dowd put it, with instrumental jams and a siege of doubts about Phil Spector's production of "Tell the Truth." It still sounded too fast, too busy, too oblivious to its own lyrical thrust. The band's British label, Polydor, was preparing to release it for airplay, but Clapton and the players never thought that it sounded like them. Their attempted remedies that day spun off into 10- and 13-minute jams.

While Clapton and his mates tried to perfect their sound, Allman again asked Dowd if it would be all right if he came by to watch a session and meet Clapton. Dowd assured him it would. He put the phone down and told Clapton that Duane Allman and this great band he'd been recording were in town.

Clapton said, "You mean that guy who plays on the back of 'Hey Jude'?"

That 50-second burst in a session behind Wilson Pickett had made Allman known to Clapton before the Allman Brothers Band was anywhere near his radar screen. The rest of the Dominos were already acquainted with Allman because he had come around often to see Delaney Bramlett when they worked for him. When Dowd told him about the Allman Brothers' Miami concert, Clapton said, "We have to go."

Dowd made the necessary calls, and he and his client musicians arrived at the benefit to find the band of six Southerners set up on a flatbed trailer. At the edge of the improvised stage, Dowd's contacts sneaked Derek and the

Dominos between a barricade and sandbags that kept the crowd at a distance—they were sent through crawling on their hands and knees so they wouldn't block anyone's view. When they were in front of the stage, they sat back, pulled their knees against their chests, and propped themselves against the sandbags.

Duane was in the middle of a solo, playing with his eyes closed. He opened them and his gaze fell on Clapton. He gaped and quit playing. The Allman Brothers' leader froze, and this went on long enough that the other players scrambled; they assumed he must have broken a string or blown an amp. The other lead guitarist, Dickey Betts, stepped out and launched another solo, covering for him. Then Betts looked down and also recognized the man Duane was staring at. Betts kept playing but wheeled around and turned his back, nonplussed. Duane Allman had not been awestruck in the presence of Wilson Pickett or Aretha Franklin, but they were not among the world's best guitar players.

Long after midnight, after the concert was over and some food consumed, a caravan of Winnebagos rolled in front of Criteria Recording and the Allman Brothers trooped into the studio with Derek and the Dominos. Like most dream jams, the cast and concept were better than the tapes that came out of it. They went off on stoned tangents and seemed to forget where they were going; at times the guitars caterwauled more than they soared. Clapton and Duane Allman at first acted as if they were a little afraid of each other. But when they overcame their shyness, they were at once teaching, learning, and sharing: "They were trading licks, they were swapping guitars," Dowd described the scene. "They were talking shop and information and having a ball—no holds barred, just admiration for each other's technique and facility. . . . They went on for 15, 18 hours like that. I went through two or three sets of engineers."

For Clapton, the jams' greatest revelation was hearing what Allman could bleed from old blues veins with his Coricidin bottle. "What really got me interested in [bottleneck] as an electric approach was seeing Duane take it to another place," he said. "There were very few people playing electric slide that were doing anything new; it was just the Elmore James licks, and everyone knows those. No one was opening it up until Duane showed up and played it a completely different way."

The rest of the Allman Brothers Band drifted off to their motel rooms, but Duane stayed on as the fifth member of Clapton's studio band. Allman said of Clapton's decisive willingness to change course: "He said, 'Okay, man. We're going to make us a record here, and we're going to have two guitar players instead of one.'" The Allman Brothers were hot and had prestigious gigs to play, but Duane could wax philosophical about art and profession, in his down-home way, and in so doing justify sticking around to play with Clapton and company. "We ain't jiving a bit when we play," he said of his band. "We ain't trying to impress anybody with our fancy clothes. We just go out and play our music— all anybody ought to do. The rock scene is a very charming thing. It's easy to get caught up in it. But it don't make any difference. It's just like raccoon coats and the Charleston. It's just a trip. But it's important that people distinguish between the trips and the music. You can appreciate a good theatrical presentation. But you've got to reserve something for the music, too—you've got to hear it."

From that very first night, Allman heard the music of

Derek and the Dominos. The band was in the studio because of Clapton's commercial stature and vision for this record, but in subtle ways Allman became a coleader of the Dominos. The next day, they heard the difference as soon as Allman's bottleneck rode in behind the inelegant grunt that for some reason kicked off "Tell the Truth." This was not going to be rock's tiresome rite of dueling guitarists—they complemented each other's play so instinctively and so well that one comfortably moved into the spaces and style of the other. On "Tell the Truth" and other pieces, Clapton overcame his qualms and contributed some of his own licks of bottleneck. "Eric is coming along on his slide," Allman later kidded him in a magazine interview. "He's doing okay. He ain't no Duane Allman of the slide guitar, but he's doing all right!" It's not a failure of the ear that sometimes it's hard to be certain which one of them is playing what on *Layla*.

After those first sessions with Allman, Clapton got on the phone to Robert Stigwood and ordered him to pull back Polydor's single release that Phil Spector had produced. He thought that if that version of "Tell the Truth" got on the radio, it would hurt the album's prospects, not help them. They had the right take on the song now.

Allman could not be there for every track on the record. He had to leave Miami for a couple of days to attend to the business of his own band. Derek and the Dominos recorded initial songs on the album—"I Looked Away" and "Bell Bottom Blues"—quite well without him. But as Dowd put it, "All of a sudden the catalyst was there. It was just a matter of putting things in shape."

His addition did not mean that they toned down their behavior. Clapton later said that they scored a massive amount of heroin and cocaine while in Florida, enough to keep them in blow while they were on tour. Whitlock said that a well-known photo of Duane, which came out of the *Layla* sessions, had him on the phone looking very business-like. "He was scoring coke and hookers," Whitlock chortled. "Not just any hookers, either. They had to be imports from Macon."

———

Though Clapton sometimes said he didn't know he was on to anything special with "Layla" or the other songs, he told Whitlock when they finished the Miami sessions that he knew this album was going to be "the epitome" of his career. "It's what you'd expect to hear a guy say when he's 70," said Whitlock, "not 25." Clapton confided to Radle once when the Dominos were touring, "If I didn't love this music, I'd hate it." He put all the creativity and passion he had into the 14 songs that made the final cut. He was drained, and he didn't know if reaching so far beyond what he'd attempted before was going to make any real difference in his life. He was thinking about his future with Pattie Boyd Harrison, not just record sales and positions on *Billboard* charts. Clapton had sold his bandmates on the sound he wanted to hear, but he also involved them in his drama and dream. None spoke of him sharing the secrets of his love of Pattie—it wasn't necessary. Every young man has a Layla in his life, or failing that, in his imagination.

When they began, they had no idea it would be a double album. They worried about having enough material to fill up one. The finished album contained nine original songs and five covers that spanned decades' worth of the music that had informed and shaped them, from Big Bill Broonzy to Jimi Hendrix. With a couple of exceptions near the start, it came together in the sequence it was recorded. That editing rarity was enhanced by the technologies pioneered by their engineer, but mainly it was the intensity of the musicians' play, which shaped the album into far more than just a loose collection of love songs. It worked like a novel structured as a book of short stories.

The first song, "I Looked Away," evokes some guy who might be in a bar, remembering how good his life was and wondering how it went so wrong. Clapton's voice sounds as if he is trying not to break into tears. Whitlock's baritone muscles in with the explanation and fatal complication, that messy old-fashioned business of loving another man's woman.

Then comes the erotic slow dance of "Bell Bottom Blues." This song contains Clapton's distinctive clear ringing notes on his Fender (you understand, hearing them, why he's famous for breaking strings) and then high, short, furious bursts of solo—Slowhand showing once more how fast he can play—with Carl Radle ambling alongside in his calm, sure, good-humored stride.

On "Bell Bottom Blues," Whitlock contributes harmony at times, but through most of the lines, he just jabs the keyboard and lets his partner sing with newfound confidence and power. The lyrics get right to the point of a serious lovers' quarrel. But Clapton departs in the phrasing to add a touch that's funny and salacious—the kind of sound a man makes when a woman's twists and shoves reminds him of the joy of just being alive. It's a blues song, though, one that Robert Johnson would have been proud to sing, can't the woman see what this affair is doing to him? Doesn't it hurt her to watch and hear him beg? Didn't it hurt her to see him beg? Here was a man stripped naked in love and pain.

"Bell Bottom Blues" is a breathtaking piece of music, and nine more of the songs to come are just as good. After that cut, Allman's play becomes a growing force on the record. Whitlock, who later joked that he was fighting for his life on his keyboard, in danger of being drowned by all the guitars, lets go a shout of triumph as they explore one of his own personal feats on the record, "Keep on Growing." Clapton and Allman had initially composed it as an instrumental, and it would have been cut from the album if Whitlock hadn't rushed out into the lobby to write the lyrics. He came back with the words in less than 20 minutes. On this one, Whitlock sings the lead and Clapton provides harmony. It's about a young man hell-bent on trouble—he had believed the sweet-talking woman who told him everything was going to work out fine, that love would find a way. The guitar duet begins with Allman playing slide, but when the singing ends, Clapton goes off on one of his characteristic high-pitched tears. Allman stays right with him, setting aside both his Coricidin bottle and the customary style of playing rhythm chords in second lead; he unleashes a note-blending flurry reminiscent of the one that made his reputation behind Wilson Pickett on "Hey Jude."

Next comes a down-and-dirty rhythm and blues song credited in 1922 to a Tin Pan Alley writer, Jimmie Cox. "Nobody Knows You When You're Down and Out" has been sung in varied versions over the years by greats including Ida Cox, Bessie Smith, Sam Cooke, John Lennon, and Janis Joplin, but Allman's sorrowful bottleneck and the bitterness and self-pity in Clapton's voice and guitar work made it their own. It's easy to believe that the man in the song will never get his hands on a dollar again. The blues standard is followed by a dramatic change of pace, with Allman's guitar playing sounding almost Persian. In a style portending another pop classic inspired by Pattie, "Wonderful Tonight," Clapton turns to a quiet and tender voice that directly links them to the story of Layla with lines adapted from and credited to the poet Nizami. "I Am Yours" removes any doubt that his album was inspired in part by his reading of the Persian epic drawn from the legend of Majnun and Layla.

The next Clapton-Whitlock song, "Anyday," is rightly hailed as one of the album's enduring rock classics. It begins with a novel pairing of Whitlock's Hammond organ and Allman's bottleneck guitar. In Gene Santoro's fine essay about the *Layla* sessions, Whitlock described Allman's impact: "Eric and I had already written it, but then Duane came up with that slide part. He said, 'Hey, check this out; let's make it like a Roman chariot race.'" This race is a long one, with constant changes of speed. It features some of the album's best Whitlock and Clapton vocal tradeoffs in the Memphis style of Sam and Dave. The song is part entreaty from the man and part assurance to his lover that someday she'll have reason to smile again. "Anyday" is an address to George Harrison: In some of the strongest writing and singing on the album, with a metaphor of breaking glass and twisting knife—intimations of someone literally tearing at his guts—Clapton voices a brutal, mocking, yet respectful challenge to the other party in the love triangle. "Anyday" maintains that only a fool brings a woman home after she's betrayed him in bed and left him for another, but if you love her enough to do that, you have really proved yourself to be a man.

———

"Key to the Highway" made it onto the record as a fluke. Born and raised in the Dallas area, the Mexican-American Domingo Samudio migrated to Memphis in the fifties, and in the midsixties as the flamboyant showman of Sam the Sham and the Pharaohs he scored two hits, "Wooly Bully" and "Li'l Red Riding Hood," each of which reached number two on the *Billboard* charts. A decade older than Derek and the Dominos, Sam the Sham was their grizzled, true blues hero. The same year as *Layla* was produced, Duane Allman played on the border rock pioneer's attempted comeback album. He may have simply walked across the hall to do it.

Criteria Recording was a busy place, and it happened that in August 1970 Samudio had booked a session there. The Dominos could hear him howling "Key to the Highway" in another studio. Clapton had loved and performed that blues song since he discovered one of its authors, Big Bill Broonzy, when he was an English village lad, and it had been one of the staples of Allman's ill-starred band Hour Glass. The guitarists started playing it, fooling around, and Whitlock and Gordon joined in. Tom Dowd was in the john when he heard what they were doing. The track laid down on *Layla* begins with Clapton well into his blues lead because Dowd realized the tape wasn't rolling. He ran out yelling, "Hit the goddamn machine!"

In the refashioned "Tell the Truth" and "Why Does Love Got to Be So Sad," the mood of the story turns resentful.

———

The interplay of Clapton and Allman almost gets away from them, but Radle and Gordon's pacing calls them back. They cover "Have You Ever Loved a Woman," the Billy Myles blues song Clapton had loved on first hearing Freddie King's version. It's an ironic choice of material—in performances of the song Clapton would work into his delivery a sly chuckle, for now the crowd is in on the joke. How could this conniving man sing about the shame and sinfulness of running off with your best friend's wife?

It's easier to empathize with pain that rises above anger. The album's tone changes abruptly with a cover of Jimi Hendrix's "Little Wing," about a girl walking through the clouds. The girl in question is, in fact, an apparition; Hendrix said that when he wrote the song, he was trying to convey the ethereal atmosphere of the pop festival in Monterey, California, in 1967. But Clapton's singing and his guitar play with Allman give the woman a face and heart and beauty, in addition to all the pain she and a man are putting each other through. Whatever Clapton's relationship with Hendrix was, he recorded "Little Wing" as a tribute to his peer, and you can sense how haunting and moving the gift was to the giver.

The next piece, also one of the album's gems, was Carl Radle's idea. Chuck Willis, a black rhythm and blues artist from Atlanta, had recorded a song called "It's Too Late" in 1956. Harking back to his Oklahoma roots, Radle heard the sway of country music in the song, and Derek and Dominos play it that way. The album's last cover song is a perfect swinging bridge between "Little Wing" and the masterpiece to come. It's too late, buddy. That girl of your dreams is gone.

Clapton's title song distills an 800-year-old, 8,000-line poem about the Muslim world's favorite love story into a very simple rock lyric. The only clear connections with Nizami's poem are the song title, "Layla," Clapton's mesmerizing agony over an unrequited love, and his utterly convincing belief that the love is driving him insane.

The lines in the song are so plainly stated, and everyone in the Western world, at least, knows the tune, yet accomplished musicians have said that it's not an easy song to learn to play. Clapton didn't work it over and over for years only to come up with "a ditty." You can break it down into its parts; the exact source of the magic still evades you. Radle lays out a sure line of bass, and his own melody never strays; Gordon bangs snare rolls at the start and end of each verse; Whitlock echoes Clapton's cries of her name, and near what he believes will be the end, the singer and credited writer or co-writer of six of the album's nine original songs shouts *"Whoop whoop whoop whoop!"* in sheer exultation.

But how would it have sounded if Allman hadn't had the brainstorm of adding that seven-note introduction, which he adapted from a riff in an old Albert King blues creation? Clapton said the song was "As the Years Go Passing By." The Memphis bluesman composed it as a slow song, but Allman greatly speeds it up. The result delivers as unforgettable a lead guitar run as "Johnny B. Goode," "Satisfaction," or "Crossroads." The lead of "Layla" would be Clapton's life-long signature, but in the studio Allman was the one who conceived and played it.

Whitlock saw Albert King on a plane just weeks before

his mentor and hero died. Whitlock remarked that the song had made quite a lot of money for Clapton (and for him as well, though he didn't say that). King said, "You tell that boy he don't owe me nothin' for that tune. I got lots of tunes."

Whitlock was disgusted by Clapton's sudden idea of using Jim Gordon's (and Rita Coolidge's) piano notion as a coda for "Layla"—he thought they already had a great rock 'n' roll song, and found this to be, in a word, phony. But Whitlock played and recorded a track of it because his friend and boss asked him to. Dowd's editing mastery made Gordon's and Whitlock's takes on the piece sound like one piano. Then Dowd patched it on, despite a technical glitch that resulted in it being recorded at three different speeds.

Elaborate essays have been written about the merits and flaws of "Layla" and the rest of the album. On the question, raised by *Guitar World* magazine of whether Allman and Clapton were playing out of tune, one critic from cyberspace put in: "The outro of 'Layla' is actually in a different key from the rest of the song—the song is in D, with a typically rock styled major-minor ambiguity. . . . With this sharpening of the piano, it's more like the song goes down by a 'blue' interval, not quite a whole step but more than a half step. . . . Going down by a blue interval is a classic part of a blues turnaround, and the outro of 'Layla' becomes a turnaround that goes on, and on, and on . . . " To which another Web critic famously responded: "The end of 'Layla' sounds like cats in heat. It is easily one of the most annoying solos ever made." Thousands more people, however, agree with Richard E. Land of Fayetteville, Arkansas, who reviewed the album for the Amazon.com Web Site: "If you like blues-based rock 'n' roll, with virtuoso guitar players on prominent display, this is the holy grail."

Clapton's instinct to add the piano coda freed Allman to explore his most expansive serenades with the plastic bottle of cold medicine: the guitars of the two stylists entwined like flowering vines, finally ending with a twitter of birds. The effect at the end was an acoustic trick Allman had come upon in his scuffling days as a session player in Muscle Shoals and New York—his tribute to the great Bird of jazz, Charlie Parker.

At the end of the sessions, Dowd told them that they might be able to work in one more song on what had evolved into a double album. "Hey, Bobby," Clapton said. "Why don't you sing that song of yours, the one about the thorn tree?" It was a generous and thoughtful thing for Clapton to do; he knew the album's last word and sentiment would belong to Whitlock, to all the Dominos, not just him. It was the song Whitlock had written in pain and loss behind the closed door of his little room at Leon Russell's Plantation in Southern California. Just as the kid had bravely predicted would happen, Derek and the Dominos recorded his song as an acoustic number, sitting in a circle with guitars around omnidirectional mikes. Thirty years later, a man would write to an online music forum: "Since the first time I heard 'Thorn Tree in the Garden' from *Layla and Other Assorted Love Songs*, I knew it was written for me. It just so completely nailed the way I felt about a particular relationship that was very profound for a 16-year-old kid. Finding out years later that the song was about a dog didn't diminish the effect or my love for the song one bit."

The song begins with the rhetorical assumption that you know what Whitlock means by this song and his metaphor of one boy's tenuous hold on earth. After the album came out, George Harrison approached Whitlock one day with a twinkle in his eye. A central figure in all this heartbreak and melodrama, he said to his friend, "But Bobby, what if I *don't* know what you mean?"

9

CAMELOT

IF ANYONE IN THE INNER CIRCLE doubted the identity and thrust of "Layla," it was not Paula Boyd. On hearing the song in Florida, she went straight back to England and moved her things out of Hurtwood Edge. Her romance with Bobby Whitlock continued for several months. Clapton meanwhile made his best pitch to Pattie. He gave her a tape of his album of love songs and a copy of Nizami's lyrical poem. Clapton begged her to quit her marriage and come away with him. Pattie was in love with Clapton—their liaison that summer had not been casual. But she also loved her husband, and she was tired of all the torment. She told Eric that what he wanted was impossible, and that it was over between them. She wouldn't leave George.

Indulging the worst of his instincts, Clapton wallowed in self-pity and bullied her emotionally. Pattie described his ultimatum: "Eric showed me this packet of heroin and said, 'Either you come away with me or I will take this.'" The clear implication was that he would keep on taking heroin, and if it killed him, it would be her fault. "I was appalled," she said. "I grabbed at it and tried to throw it away, but he snatched it back. I turned him down—and, for 4 years, he became a heroin addict.

"At first, I felt guilt. Then I felt anger because it was totally irrational of him to blame me for something he was probably going to do anyway; it was very selfish and destructive."

Clapton was extremely bitter: "The only thing that meant anything to me was 'Layla,' which was because it was actually about an emotional experience, a woman that I felt deeply about and that turned me down, and I had to kind of pour it out in some way. So we wrote these songs, made an album, and the whole thing was great. She didn't give a damn."

Pattie was hardly indifferent to what he'd accomplished in *Layla*. "I think he was incredibly raw at the time," she said later. "He's such an incredible musician that he's able to put his emotions into music in such a way that the audience can feel it instinctively. It goes right through you."

She loved him, but she was not willing to give herself up to his fantasy and obsessions. Harrison, for his part, had realized the night he was finishing his solo album that Eric was sleeping with Pattie. And then when she came home from the *Oh! Calcutta!* party at Stigwood's estate, he had the nerve to call her in the middle of the night and sweet-talk her for an hour. The cuckold of Esher could see that Clapton had come unhinged. He probably wasn't physically afraid of what Clapton might do, but if the ex-Beatle was the winner in this mess, it could only have been a sense of triumph that tasted like gall. George at once got his wife out of Eric's close range, taking her to romantic Henley in the Thames River valley. Clapton continued living with the diplomat's daughter, and incredibly, according to the Christopher Sandford biography, *Edge of Darkness*, he moved in on his pal Whitlock and took another spin with Paula Boyd.

The band had no time to unwind and regroup. On September 11th, the day after they finished the sessions in Miami, they had a performance date at the trusty old Marquee in London. After a week's pause, they were then looking at 42 concerts in Britain and the States, dates for a tour that would last into December, when *Layla* would be formally released. At Hurtwood Edge, Clapton learned that Jimi Hendrix had finished a tour of Europe and was taking a break in London. He had just played a concert in Germany in which a crowd booed and taunted him. Sting, Stevie Ray Vaughan, and many other artists would pay tribute to "Little Wing" over the years, but none captured its spirit better than Derek and the Dominos. Clapton wanted to deliver his gift personally to Hendrix and be there when he heard the recording.

They made plans to get together on the 18th at a Sly and the Family Stone show at the Lyceum. An avid shopper, Clapton went out and got another present for Hendrix. The left-handed American had adapted by learning to play a standard guitar upside down. In a West End shop, Clapton found a rare Stratocaster made for left-handers. He bought the Fender and planned to give it to Hendrix that night, but somehow they never made the connection. And Hendrix never got to hear Clapton's version of "Little Wing." At a London hotel in the early morning hours of the 18th, he died choking from an overdose of the powerful downer Vesperax.

The police and ambulance crew found the door of the hotel room wide open. His girlfriend was gone.

Clapton did not attend the funeral. He was already an emotional wreck, and he feared a circus of microphones and cameras. One acquaintance said he wept for 15 hours. Another said his grief was tied to his own ego: He felt Hendrix had left him to carry the load by himself.

A month after the *Layla* album wrapped up, Duane Allman put on earphones in a New York radio station in an ebullient mood. "Hello. Everybody out there in radio land, take off your underwear, relax, and let ol' Duane tell you just how it is." The disc jockey, who must have been delighted with this outburst, asked him how he was getting along. "I'm drunk, man. I feel good, man. Let's talk. Man, I've been doing bunches of D-O-P-E and acting C-R-A-Z-Y and all the other stuff you can't talk about on the air."

Idlewild South, the album Tom Dowd had been producing and engineering for the Allman Brothers when Stigwood called about Clapton's new record and band, came out that fall. A *Rolling Stone* reviewer called the Southerners' second album "a big step forward" and said one cut, "In Memory of Elizabeth Reed," was "stupendous." The *New York Times* called the record "exciting and bold," and it exceeded sales expectations, reaching number 38 on the *Billboard* charts. *Idlewild South* prompted Bill Graham's operation to book the band the following spring—the double album that came out of that gig, *At Fillmore East,* would make them superstars, the hottest band in America. Duane's experience with

Derek and the Dominos was just one of the good things in the mix of his life, and it was not the major one. But the artistic and personal connection he'd made with Clapton was profound. Allman was still riding the incredible high of what they'd accomplished, and getting back to his own business, the Allman Brothers Band was truly smokin', after years of struggle and disappointment.

A couple of weeks after Duane's effusive radio interview in New York, the road took the Allman Brothers to their birthplace, Nashville. They participated in a rowdy jam that night, and then Duane helped himself to repeated helpings of tar opium. The plan was to get a jump on the road and roll on through the black morning hours after they caught a little nap. The person sent to rouse Duane couldn't wake him up. Allman was a notoriously hard sleeper—the Atlantic producer Jerry Wexler had once sent his little boy into his guest bedroom with a trumpet to wake Duane up. But this time there was nothing funny about it. His lips and fingertips were blue.

At the emergency room, the musicians couldn't believe their ears. "We'll do what we can," a doctor said, "but there's not much hope. He's pretty far gone." But in time, the doctor reappeared and said that Duane had come out of it. He was going to be all right. It was a very close call.

Dowd spent that month mixing *Layla*, and the band came back to Miami for some overdubbing, which led to one more set-to between Clapton and Dowd. After hearing the mix, the star complained that the vocals were too loud. "You don't realize," Dowd argued, "that your record is going to get played on the radio alongside Mick Jagger—whomever—and the vocal has to be out in front." Besides, he thought the insecure star was becoming a first-rate singer. They didn't decide to add the coda to Layla until the last minute. "When we finished it and were mastering it," Dowd said, "I felt it was the best goddamned album I'd been involved with since *The Genius of Ray Charles*."

Atlantic's executives and marketing chiefs agreed with Dowd, though in England Stigwood and Polydor's chiefs were skittish. Stigwood ordered the printing of several thousand badges that read: "Derek Is Eric." Hoping to jump-start the airplay, they decided to single release the so-called rock version of "Layla" without Gordon's coda, with "Bell Bottom Blues" as the B-side. Right after that decision was made, Ed Leimacher's advance review of the album in *Rolling Stone* called it "one hell of a record" but also said it was padded with fillers like "Have You Ever Loved a Woman" and "Bell Bottom Blues." "Nesuhi and Ahmet Ertegun and Jerry Wexler were absolutely enamored of the album," Dowd said of Atlantic's partners, "but they couldn't get the goddamn thing on the air; they couldn't get a single out of it. Nothing. I kept walking around talking to myself for a year. Then suddenly it was the national anthem."

"Layla" became a cult item and backdoor hit when FM disc jockeys in the States discovered and started airing the 7-minute version. While they waited for the world to start applauding their feat, the musicians had not been sitting reading the comics. They were staying high and working hard. Neither the British nor the American label poured advertising into the album's promotion, but both supported the tour. In the United Kingdom, Derek and the Dominos stormed Croydon, Leicester, Brighton, Liverpool, Glasgow, Bristol, Manchester, Birmingham, Bournemouth, Scarborough, and on October 11 the Lyceum Ballroom, where the band first took on the name Derek and the Dominos. Across the Atlantic, they played Rider College in Trenton, New Jersey; George Washington University in Washington, D.C.; and then two nights, October 23rd and 24th, at the Fillmore East in New York.

To Bobby Whitlock, life didn't seem bad: In fact, he couldn't figure how it could get much better. "In New York one night I came in and said, 'I just signed a record contract on the hood of a car! Eric said, 'You did *what?*' It was for $9,000. I hadn't had $9,000 in my life." (Whitlock's first solo records, *Bobby Whitlock* and *Raw Velvet,* would come out on ABC Dunhill. For *One of a Kind* and *Rock Your Sox Off,* he subsequently moved to Capricorn, the label Atlantic had created to develop and promote the Allman Brothers—which deepened Whitlock's affiliation with Southern rock, though he continued to live in England and, for a while, Ireland.) Now, if he needed to go somewhere, he just called a limo. He was too green to know that very meticulous books were being kept on those expenditures and they would be charged against the album's net. He just knew he was having a lot of fun.

Whitlock did notice that twice as many mikes as he was used to seeing were on the stage at the Fillmore East. He didn't stop to think that through; he attributed it to the class of the place, which had handsome architecture and marvelous acoustics and was in the heart of Greenwich Village. But while one set of mikes was wiring their play to their monitors and the crowd, the other went to a sound truck or room where tapes were rolling. Someone was recording a second

Derek and the Dominos album—only the band hadn't been informed of it.

Allman was busy elsewhere with his band's own concert schedule, but Whitlock thought their Fillmore dates were as good as Derek and the Dominos ever played. A clean-shaven Clapton came out wearing a sharp white sport coat and dark shirt with yellow polka dots over his jeans. One reviewer in New York thought Clapton's play was listless. Another maintained that Whitlock banged away on his piano off-key. There was a good deal of impatience with Jim Gordon's 6-minute drum solo in "Let It Rain." You have to give him credit, though: The guy could play, and he was in *shape*. Despite the shrugs of the New York critics, the crowd responded as if they had heard those shows the way the musicians thought they played them. They were dancing, hopping up and down, from the start.

J. D. Smith is now a musician and radio host in San Francisco. He was then a student at Millburn High School in New Jersey and a Clapton fan who had seen two concerts of Cream and the disastrous Blind Faith concert in Madison Square Garden. His review of a Derek and the Dominos concert at the Fillmore, which was later published on a Clapton Web site, provides a sense of the atmosphere that night—and why this music just exploded, especially in Americans' consciousness, and why it still revs up listeners 35 years later.

"Since it was the late show," Smith wrote, "we had to stand outside and wait for the second show, which started at 11:00 p.m. That was part of the magic of New York; all the great shows of any concerts, jazz or rock, started at 11:00 or later. I believe that WNEW-FM and WPLJ-FM, the two biggest progressive rock stations in New York at the time, had been airing at least three cuts from the upcoming album, *Layla*. And when I heard them, I was blown away. The songs were beautiful. The voices were almost ungodly. I remember standing outside the theater waiting while the first show went on, and about every 2 or 3 minutes someone would be opening up the side exit door and this incredible sound with Clapton in the forefront would be blazing out."

One of the opening acts was Humble Pie, the band of the guitarist Peter Frampton. At last the time came for Clapton's mysterious new band. "Hardly anyone knew what they were about," Smith wrote, "and no one probably had a clue what was going on with Clapton's personal life at that time. The first song was 'Got to Get Better in a Little While'—as hard and driving a song as I'd ever heard. It was like nothing Clapton had ever done before. You could tell the Delaney and Bonnie influence, except it was more refined and defined."

The first time Clapton saw Hendrix play, he was awed that anyone could play lead and rhythm parts at once. But that's what Clapton was doing now. They went into "Little Wing," which was a pleasant surprise to the crowd, for the Hendrix cover had not yet received airplay. Then, of even greater surprise to the band, Whitlock's organ froze up like a computer. It just groaned and swooned. Radle dipped his knees and followed the sound down, and they played through the crisis as if it were part of the plan. Clapton, Radle, and Gordon hunkered down and became a trio, producing echoes of Cream. "This was the best concert I'd ever seen," the teenage Smith wrapped up his piece. "I was soaked from head to toe. I had been to church. And one other thing: On the record, at the end of 'Got To Get Better In A Little While' before Clapton plays that last E (ninth) chord, you can hear this loud yell of sheer delight. That was me. I was there!"

In Nashville, on November 5, they got to appear on Johnny Cash's TV show. Carl Radle was trying to squire Clapton out to a studio to meet and play with J. J. Cale, but that particular meeting of minds and artistic temperaments had to await another cross of the roads. For Cash's program, they decided they'd better play "It's Too Late" because it was the only cut on *Layla* that was passably country. (They should have known that Cash wouldn't care; they wound up getting to play several songs with the man in black and Carl Perkins, a joyous experience for the youths.) When everything was ready, Cash began his intro, "And we're pleased to have a new band from London, Derek and the Dominos."

Whitlock couldn't help himself. "We're not from London!" he cried. "I'm from Memphis, that guy's from Tulsa, that one's from California. There's only one of us from London."

Cash gave out a bark of laughter and said to the camera crew, "Okay, cut, cut—we'll have to do that one over."

———

Halfway through the tour, the band seemed to be on top of their game. But fatigue was setting in, and the drugs and booze were taking their physical and psychological toll; troubling self-doubts and conflicts began to intrude, and everything swirled around the mercurial experience and mood of Clapton. "One time," Whitlock said, "I walked in a motel room and Carl Radle was sacked out with five good-looking women. I thought, *all right*. I always thought that what broke up that band was too many drugs and not enough women."

Asked to explain, Whitlock said, "Well, from the start I

had a particular problem with our manager. I'd been abused once by a man when I was a kid, and I didn't like being propositioned. Of course, I didn't have to see Robert Stigwood all the time. But Jim Gordon had a way of making me feel very uncomfortable. The way we set up on stage, he and I were looking right at each other. We'd be playing up a storm, and he'd be mouthing about certain things he'd like to do with me. I thought they both needed to see a damn doctor. But that was Jim. He liked to swing both ways."

Whitlock was offended by the perceived passes, and he didn't appreciate feeling trapped under a spotlight while he was trying to play. Of course, he could have talked to his longtime friend if they had a serious problem, but all the Dominos were getting paranoid and rattled. Suddenly it wasn't the band chemistry they had loved when they were playing those tiny joints in England. "Eric was going through such a bad time," Whitlock went on. "On top of everything with Pattie, he fell in love with the wife of a black jazz musician, a famous one. In New York he took her on a major shopping spree. You wouldn't believe. He asked me, 'How do you think it'd be if I took her back to England?' 'Well, gee, Eric, how would I know?' But he decided that's what he wanted to do. Then she told him, 'You owe me $5,000.' '*Owe* you?' Eric said. He was in love with this woman, and she was a hooker, playing him for a fool. He threw the money in her face. It was just one crushing blow after another."

In early November, right after the Johnny Cash show, the tour was heading out West when Clapton got a call from Stigwood that his grandfather had fallen critically ill. He rushed back to Surrey to witness suffering in his family and bury the old tradesman he considered to be his father. *Layla and Other Assorted Love Songs* came out in December, just as the tour came to a close, and it encountered the same maddening quiet as the single release had. If Clapton and his American friends had done something extraordinary, there was very little awareness of it at that time. Clapton's former boss John Mayall remarked in an interview that appeared the month the album debuted: "He's got a little outfit on the road now. And that's the first time he's taken it in his head to throw out all the superstar categories, get a band together, and play gigs for small money just for the sake of playing in small clubs. It is really commendable." Mayall's remark probably referred to the tour Clapton and the band had launched 6 months earlier, but it was characteristic of the strange hole their work had fallen into. Clapton had delivered the most heartfelt music of his career, but the public perception largely seemed to be: *Wonder what happened to that guy who used to play with Cream?*

Bobby Whitlock's self-titled solo debut, which would be released in 1972, was soul with a drawl and bite of country and gospel, the Southern-roots rock genre that was fast catching on. Once more, Derek and the Dominos (minus Duane Allman) were the core studio band. Band relationships were dicey enough, though, that they did not all play together. Whitlock had evidently gotten over his annoyance with Gordon. At the Olympic Sound Studios in London, they recorded the base track of his solo album, *Bobby Whitlock,* in January 1971, just the two of them. Radle and Clapton came in and played their parts later. "Duane's influence on Eric," Whitlock observed, "was so strong that you heard Eric on that record and at times you thought it was Duane." George Harrison also came in the studio to play guitar. But Whitlock's keyboard play and the horn tandem of his Delaney and Bonnie pals Jim Price and Bobby Keys were more prominent than the lead guitars. Opening with "Where There's a Will, There's a Way," the tune Bobby had written with Bonnie Bramlett, he sings the soul material as if he is yearning to be Gregg Allman, but he doesn't quite have the pipes; those songs sound, oddly, as if he misses singing with Clapton.

Bobby Whitlock was coproduced by the artist and Andy Johns, a veteran of Rolling Stones recordings. It ended with his song "Back Home in England," but the best cuts of his album with the Dominos as his studio band were homesick songs that drew on his roots in country-western and gospel music—"A Day without Jesus," "The Dreams of a Hobo," and "I'd Rather Live the Straight Life"—in which a young man swears that he'd rather be cold-turkey straight in Memphis than the junkie he was in Los Angeles. Straining to be optimistic is his "Song for Paula." The cover opens like a book—though it's not a double album—and for the photo shoot Pattie's sister posed beside him seated in a forest, looking as uncertain as he sounded on some of the songs.

A better record, also released in 1972, is the sequel *Raw Velvet*. The session musicians are varied, but the imprint of *Layla* is still strong: It begins with Bobby demonstrating how "Tell the Truth" can be played and sung in a fast, jumpy roots-rock style and still work lyrically. Another high point is "Hello L.A., Bye Bye Birmingham," written by Delaney Bramlett and Mac Davis; with domino graphics, Bobby signals on the cover that Clapton and Gordon helped in the studio on that song, though they are not formally credited.

Bobby finds the solo voice he unveiled on "Thorn Tree" in another love song, "Dearest, I Wonder," which he wrote with Paula Boyd. A record company ad promoting the first album and a single, "Ease Your Pain," which was included on *Raw Velvet,* sported a photo of him with shoulder-length locks and proclaimed, "Before you ever heard of Bobby Whitlock, several rock stars heard of him first."

"Ah, yes," he would say, looking back. "My days as the young prince."

After helping Whitlock on his solo albums—and playing some fine country guitar—Clapton overdubbed some parts for a reunion album that John Mayall was putting together; then, in April, Derek and the Dominos returned to the Olympic studios to record a second album, this time without Tom Dowd. They cut a less spirited version of "Got to Get Better in a Little While" and tracks called "Moody Jam," "Jim's Song," and "Carl and Me." None of them had *Layla's* fire and passion.

Whitlock didn't know what was going on in Gordon's mind—or in Clapton's or Radle's or, for that matter, in his own. The heroin and booze and coke had caught up with all of them. Even in that state an astute businessman, Gordon wanted more of the songwriting royalties in return for giving up the piano piece for "Layla." He also had a great deal to say. Whitlock, who was hardly devoid of ego, bit his tongue to keep from reminding Gordon that he was just the *drummer;* Derek and the Dominos already had a proven songwriting team. The studio sessions were dominated by dickering and bickering between Clapton and Gordon. "The stuff we were doing was clever," Whitlock scorned the new material. "I didn't understand it, and I didn't like playing it."

Still, Whitlock didn't want to lose Derek and the Dominos. In the studio one day in May 1971, Gordon carefully tuned each component of a new and elaborate drum set, playing off a piano note provided by Whitlock. Clapton was tuning up at the same time. They were all wrecked from the way they'd been living, and they may well have been under the influence at that precise moment. The ongoing sound was monotony, and they were bored and irritable, which exacerbated the animus that had been building between Clapton and Gordon. Clapton made a complimentary remark about the drummer in a band called the Dixie Flyers that was appearing in London. Among other credits, the Dixie Flyers played with Rita Coolidge.

Gordon snapped a reply at the superstar.

"I don't remember making the remark," Clapton later described the exchange, "but he got up behind the kit and said, 'Why don't you get so-and-so in here? He could play it better than I could.'"

Clapton's face flushed, he made a sharp retort, and he went on twisting the pegs on the headstock of his guitar. As Whitlock recalled it, the flashpoint came when Gordon offered, "Would you like me to tune that thing for you?"

Oh, Christ, thought Whitlock. Here it goes . . . and he was right.

Suddenly the band leader and drummer were raging at each other. Clapton unstrapped his guitar, and according to Whitlock, in getting it off he slung it around wildly enough to deck someone. He slammed it to the floor and yelled at Gordon: "I'll never play with you again."

10

VICTIMS AND SURVIVORS

DUANE ALLMAN NEVER HYPED his role in the making of *Layla and Other Assorted Love Songs*. When "Layla" finally started playing on the radio, in the company of friends he would poke his chest on hearing the seven-note lead and say, "That's my lick." But his emphasis was on the teamwork and tightness of the band. He got impatient with the inquiries of press and strangers. "For anybody who don't know and cares enough about it to know that, I play the Gibson, Eric plays the Fender. If you can tell between a Gibson and a Fender, then you'll know who played what." During the Dominos' tour, Duane was able to be where they were only a handful of times. He caught up with them one night in Tampa. Some in the audience thought Allman wasn't at his best—maybe his guitar was out of tune. But then the band went into "Have You Ever Loved a Woman," and suddenly Whitlock, Radle, and Gordon just stopped: several moments of unrecorded magic ensued between two brilliant guitarists paying tribute to each other.

In the marketplace *Layla* lagged well behind the Allman Brothers' live recording, *At Fillmore East*, which Tom Dowd had engineered in March 1971, just weeks before the Dominos broke up. That fall, Duane spent a week in New York with his friend John Hammond, a gifted Southern rocker whose father, the elder John Hammond, was the storied producer who first signed Count Basie and Aretha Franklin. Then Allman decided he'd go home to Macon and take an overdue and well-deserved vacation. He had bought another Harley-Davidson. On the Indian summer afternoon of October 29, he went for a ride. The driver of a flatbed truck turned left across a road in front of him—and abruptly stopped, still in the intersection, because the side street was unpaved. Instead of laying his new bike down Duane tried to veer around the truck, but he clipped something on its rear, his helmet went bouncing on the pavement, and he was on the street, skidding, with the Harley on top of him. It gouged the pavement and finally stopped beside a curb. People who ran to help him thought his injuries didn't look that bad—that he was just scraped up—but he had severe internal injuries that included a ruptured coronary artery. Duane Allman died 3 hours later. He was 24.

150

———

After the breakup of the Dominos, Bobby Whitlock was one of rock 'n' roll's most dedicated bad boys.

Whitlock pursued his solo career, threw around the *Layla* money that came his way, and sat in with the Stones (uncredited but documented) in the wild sessions of *Exile on Main Street*. One Sunday when he was driving home to his house in Ascot, he cut through the lovely greenbelt called the Great Park. There was a lot of traffic, all of it in his lane. Nobody coming, nobody passing—they were just creeping along beside Windsor Lake. So he took off, slamming his Porsche into third gear, fourth, fifth. Whitlock was roaring past cars when suddenly he saw some carriages out front—a white carriage and a black carriage, teams of horses to match, and on top they had some guys with feathers in their hats. The horses were rearing up against their harnesses. Whitlock figured there was nothing to do but tear around them and just go on.

He had barely arrived home when he got a call from a detective sergeant who had come to know him through other incidents requiring police jurisdiction, though no arrests had been made. The sergeant said, "Bobby, the next time you pull a stunt like that, I'm going to throw you out of the country."

Whitlock replied, "What? What'd I do?"

"You passed the Queen of England!"

The rich American hippie had disrespected the British monarchy, and the police didn't like it.

"The Queen!" Whitlock cried. "That was the *Queen?* I didn't know! If I'd known, I would've honked!"

Though the Dominos were history, *Layla* had caught on big in the States, and Clapton still exerted a powerful influence on his songwriting partner. One day in 1973, Whitlock opened up a *Rolling Stone* and read that a Derek and the Dominos live album had shipped gold, which meant that it was already a million seller—and it was just getting to the stores. *What live album?* Whitlock thought. Then he read the news item further and remembered the excess of microphones on the stage of the Fillmore East. A double live album had been recorded without the band's knowledge.

Whitlock took the magazine to the financial controller of the Robert Stigwood Organization. "I got a record out," he announced, "and I need some dough."

"How much do you need?" the controller asked, after confirming the musician's claim.

"Twenty thousand pounds."

"All right," said the man. "When do you need it?"

"Right now."

Sure enough, a guy came out and dropped £20,000 on Whitlock, who called a limo service to take him to a Ferrari dealer in downtown London. Eric had a 1972 blue Daytona Ferrari, and Bobby wanted one exactly like it. He had to go to two dealers to find a salesman who'd even talk to him. He said, "I want that blue Daytona. How much is it?"

The salesman replied, "Ten thousand seven hundred and fifty pounds."

"Get it insured," Whitlock ordered him. "I'm paying cash money for it, right now."

But the Ferrari didn't quite fit Whitlock—he was too short. He took it back and had them move the seat forward 2 inches and raise it 1½. He actually expected a little more fine-tuned engineering from a Ferrari dealer, whose mechanics just drilled holes in the floorboard and connected it with nuts, bolts, and washers. There was a little lever beside the seat, and if he accidentally tapped it, shifting gears, the seat slammed all the way back. It happened to him twice in one day. Whitlock thought, *Damn, I've got to be careful and get that fixed.*

Whitlock was prosperous enough then that he had a burly Samoan employee who ran errands, fixed things, and was a bodyguard (if need for one arose) and all-around friend. Whitlock hung out all the time with Keith Moon, the great drummer for the Who. (When Moon overdosed in London in 1978, the official ruling was "accidental misadventure.") Whitlock got home with his new Ferrari that day; shortly afterward, Moon called and said, "Why don't you come over tonight?"

So he jumped in the Daytona with the Samoan and went over. They were playing music and gobbling blue meanies, and Moon was running around, putting on different outfits. It was 4:30 a.m. when Whitlock said, "Man, I've got to go back to the house."

There wasn't any traffic, and he relished the feel of his Ferrari. He thought he was going about 160 miles an hour when he came out of third gear. When he shifted, his hand hit the lever, and the seat shot all the way back! Whitlock couldn't reach the brake pedal or anything else with his feet. He was trying to hang on and steer. The right front tire got over on the shoulder, and the car spun around three times.

"We went through a light pole," Whitlock described the crash, "then mowed down a brick wall, and at the end of the wall we uprooted a 40-foot-tall pine tree. The car nosedived, then took to the air, and did one-and-a-half flips, with a twist. We flew completely over this guy's lawn and landed in the garden, facing where we'd come from, over on the side, with the door panels buried in the ground.

"It seemed to be happening real slow. *Boom! . . . Bam! . . . Chsshh! . . . Chsshh!* Please, just make this stop. When it was finally over, the car looked like somebody had stomped on a beer can. The speedometer was stuck on 155 kilometers an hour. And there was this awful smell. Blood, gasoline, brake fluid, and, you know it when you smell it—death."

He said to his Samoan friend, "I'm sorry, I'm so sorry."

The employee mumbled, "You didn't do it."

Somehow, death had grabbed at them and missed. Whit-lock's teeth were shattered, and a piece of trim had gone through his arm. He pulled it out as if it were an arrow. He had two cracked ribs, and that was all. But it occurred to him that they were sitting on 28 gallons of gasoline. A guy came running from a house and pulled him out, and there was a sound like people *ululating*—the wheels were still going around. Whitlock's personal economy then was all cash. He always carried about £500 and kept it in a box in his car, in case he ran short.

"I looked up," he said, "and floating in the breeze, waft-ing back and forth, were all these £10 notes."

It was like a Disney movie, but this one wasn't funny.

Shortly after the wake-up Ferrari crash, he went back to Memphis, put a band together, and started playing beer joints. He stayed in hotels so squalid that he had to step around junkies' castoff needles. "In Louisiana," he said, "I played beer joints with pool tables right in front of the mikes. I did not give a shit. A message had gotten through to me: 'Just let me live.' What I was doing in England was crazy. It was not where I was supposed to be."

During Clapton's years of seclusion, his management explained that he was just engaged in a retrospective, taking a break. But the superstar had become a junkie. Harrison, who was desperately trying to help a friend in trouble, per-suaded him to fly to New York and play in the Concert for Bangladesh in Madison Square Garden in August 1971. Clapton later described his experience that week: "So I arranged by long-distance phone calls that there'd be something there for me because my heroin habit was going strong. So I fly over there and there's nothing there and we can't score . . . the only thing people seem to take in New York is smack cut by 95 percent . . . they have to shoot it up in order to get any buzz.

"I wasn't into that. I really didn't want to go that far and so it was just a question of lying on this hotel bed going through agony with people going out trying to get stronger and stronger stuff each time. All of it was like talcum powder." A cameraman came up with some methadone he'd been prescribed as a painkiller. It enabled Clapton to play the concert, but he said, on seeing the tapes, "I think I played so badly. It wasn't me at all. I just wasn't there."

Apart from a walk-on appearance in a Leon Russell concert and a studio session for a Stevie Wonder record—both in London—for the rest of 1971, 1972, and 1973, he holed up at Hurtwood Edge with Alice, both of them addicted to heroin. They did visit Keith Richards at his home in the south of France, but they seldom ventured out, except for bizarre parties with, of all people, George and Pattie Harrison. George had taken an interest in Alice, according to the Christopher Sandford book *Edge of Darkness;* Eric likened the intrigue—which did not succeed in getting them all in bed—to a popular 1969 movie about spouse swapping, *Bob and Carol and Ted and Alice.* He built model airplanes and ate chocolate and pastries. He had possessed a great deal of money, but a lot of cash was required to obtain heroin of the strength and purity needed to feed a habit by sniffing lines of it cocaine-fashion; soon he was selling things to pay for the drugs. Lord Harlech was beside himself. He wrote Clapton fatherly love letters, which drew hostile replies, and he threatened at one point to get the law after them if they didn't straighten up. A friend of the diplomat said, "It was the hardest job of David's life. And the worst. Negotiating with Kennedy was simple by comparison."

Lord Harlech finally put them in touch with Meg Patterson, a Scottish doctor who had devised a radical treatment for addiction that employed neuroelectric acupuncture. The therapy included a ban on booze and a suggested temporary separation from Alice. George Patterson, the doctor's husband and a former missionary, found it remarkable in his diagnosis and psychological profile that a village boy in England was consumed by three things: hostility toward his mother, ambition to be the earth's best blues guitar player, and the desire to lay 1,000 women." The therapists took him into their house for extended therapy, and according to the Sandford biography, one fast-starting morning, Meg Patterson asked him to make the coffee himself. The world's best guitar player replied, "Meg, I don't know how to make coffee."

In January 1973, Pete Townshend orchestrated two Rainbow Concerts to celebrate Britain's joining the rest of Western Europe in the Common Market, and he recruited a band to back up Clapton's return in those concerts. The band rehearsed at the house of the other lead guitarist, the Rolling Stones' Ron Wood. Others in the band included, from the Blind Faith days, Stevie Winwood on keyboards and vocals and Rich Grech on bass. And the drummer was the former Tulsan Jimmy Karstein, who had tormented young Bobby Whitlock by disposing of the dog that inspired "Thorn Tree in the Garden."

Clapton had put on weight on his diet of junk food and

sweets. He was nervous because his suit didn't fit, and the audience for the first show included Harrison, Ringo Starr, Elton John, and Joe Cocker. But the Rainbow Concerts went well for the singer and guitarist. On a Welsh farm owned by Alice's brother, Clapton then spent several weeks baling hay and chopping wood. The Pattersons urged Clapton not to sleep with Alice for a while, and in the process of facing up to who he was, the former Derek convinced Alice that his love for Pattie was too strong to overcome. Clapton and Ormsby-Gore kicked their heroin habits, but at the cost of their relationship.

Clapton opened few letters that came his way but in late 1973 read two from Carl Radle. His friend and bass player sent words of encouragement and hopes they'd play together again. Clapton wrote back: "Maintain loose posture—stay in touch." Radle sent his friend some tapes of what he'd been doing: country rock, the Tulsa sound.

Radle's influence led to a new backup band, a dramatic musical redirection by Clapton, and an album that would prove a resounding success: *461 Ocean Boulevard*. In April 1974, lectured by his management to stop the financial bleeding and get back to work, Clapton played a gig at the China Garden in London's Soho. Afterward, Robert Stigwood held a grand party at his house to celebrate Clapton's comeback. Clapton showed up at the party in an ugly mood, determined to force the issue with his real-life Layla.

"I'm in love with your wife," Eric announced to George, who was hardly unaware of this. "What are you going to do about it?"

"Whatever you like, man," Harrison shot back. "It doesn't worry me. You can have her and I'll have your girlfriend."

Shocked, Pattie ran away from both of them, but that was hardly the end of it. As Pete Townshend told the story, that same month he was at the Harrisons' house one night, talking to George, while in another room Eric was trying to convince Pattie to leave her husband.

According to Townshend, the former Beatle left the room where they'd been talking for a moment. Clapton stuck his head in and hissed, "I need another hour."

"What?" said Townshend.

"I need another hour before you go."

Clapton got the extra time he needed, and this time Pattie agreed to go with him. The divorce papers weren't filed, but her marriage to Harrison was over.

In public at least, Harrison was remarkably serene about his part in the love triangle. "I'm friends with Eric—really," he told *Rolling Stone* when news of the affair became public. "I'd rather she be with him than some dope."

Townshend later marveled about Clapton: "He actually straightened himself out from being a junkie, and then he went out and made his fantasy happen." Pattie moved in with Clapton. She and George divorced in 1977, and 2 years later in Tucson, where the band was touring, Eric got his wish and married her just after his 34th birthday.

But they had no immediate honeymoon. He had imposed a rule that no spouses or lovers could go on the road with his band, and she was sent home. At the end of the tour, Clapton decided that he wanted a new band. According to the Michael Schumacher biography *Crossroads*, Clapton had been dissatisfied with their playing for a year; he thought their boozing on the road had gotten out of hand, though he was soused all the time himself; and they were never completely his mates, when you got down to it, because he was British and they were all Americans.

He fired them all by telegram, and for Carl Radle it was devastating. Radle played briefly with Peter Frampton, then went back to his hometown in Oklahoma. He died in 1980, at 38, of kidney complications brought on by too many years of abusing alcohol and heroin. His gold records were reported circulating in Tulsa pawnshops.

For Eric and Pattie it was a stormy 6-year marriage, marked by mansions, fast cars, and tabloid headlines. It went the way of his addiction to alcohol, their disappointment at being unable to have a child, the pressure of just too much history, perhaps. She would tell this story about the worst of their times together. "One Christmas, I'd cooked lunch and most people had arrived and I couldn't find Eric. It was snowing outside, and I went out and called him, but I couldn't find him and became concerned. I just imagined him stumbling around in the garden. Anything could have happened." She said they found him in a stupor on a log pile in the basement. Still, when they did finally call it quits, one of the reasons he cited was that he was sober now and she still liked to drink.

Pattie left Clapton when she discovered that he had had an affair with a young Italian actress and model, Lory Del Santo. In an interview, Del Santo claimed that early in their relationship, Clapton called and said, "Hey, I'm in town."

"Which town?" she replied.

"Milan."

She asked him why he was in the city where she lived, and he replied, "Because I love you."

Pattie gave up on her marriage to Eric when she further

---

learned that her husband and Del Santo were the parents of a son. In 1991 the child, Conor, slipped through a window left open by a housecleaner and fell 53 floors to his death from a Manhattan skyscraper. The accident was mourned throughout the world in Clapton's song "Tears in Heaven."

Following the blowup with Clapton, Jim Gordon was no less the brilliant drummer. "The producers wouldn't pay me for 'Layla,'" he later complained, "because they said I would be dead in 6 months anyway." Whether that was actually said or not, Bobby Whitlock told the same story, verbatim, about alleged remarks about their life expectancy from the Stigwood agency. Gordon got married again, to a beautiful, dark-haired songwriter named Renee Armand, whom he met in San Francisco. She would have a solid career as a backup singer with John Denver, Hoyt Axton, Aaron Neville, and others of that rank, and for 2 years, right after *Layla,* she was a solo artist for A&M Records. Because of both her looks and her voice, Armand was likened to Carly Simon. Her album *The Rain Book,* which her husband produced, and for which he played most of the backup instruments, was a *New York Times* Critic's Pick in 1973. One of her most affecting songs was "Friends," a disturbing tale about a drug addict's resistance to intervention.

Twelve years later, in *Rolling Stone,* the journalist Barry Rehfeld described the unraveling life of a great musician. Jim Gordon's second marriage ended in divorce after just 6 months. One day, Armand claimed, she came home with groceries in her arms and was chilled by the kind of stare that had once terrified Rita Coolidge.

"I know what you're doing," Gordon said.

She said she didn't know what he was talking about. He pointed to three objects on the floor and said, "The magic triangle." The triangle, he went on, was evidence of evil spirits she brought into the house. When she replied that this was crazy, he threw a body punch that broke several of her ribs.

"I loved him very much," Armand said. "I didn't know what happened to him, but I couldn't stay after that."

In his career Gordon was still banging away in sessions for Johnny Rivers, Steely Dan, Maria Muldaur, Carly Simon, the Byrds, Harry Nilsson, John Lennon, and, again, George Harrison. For a while he was in the road band of Frank Zappa. Gordon bought another Ferrari in California, and like Whitlock, he totaled it. But Gordon clearly had far worse problems than reckless driving.

His friend and mentor from the days of the Wrecking Crew, Carol Kaye, said that he called once in those years, full of regret for drinking so much and for losing his teen sweetheart and first wife, Jill, the mother of his child. "Jim said, 'I was so mixed up,'" Kaye recalled, then added her conjecture: "I think what happened to him was because of all the drugs. When he was doing so well as a session musician, in those days you didn't even see a beer in the studios. Jim wasn't cut out to be a rock 'n' roll road musician."

It was more than vodka and heroin. Gordon was increasingly tormented by voices in his head—the calling card of schizophrenia. Rehfeld wrote that by 1977, Gordon was consumed by the voice of his mother, Osa Marie Gordon. The career nurse kept trying to get him psychiatric help, and over a 6-year period, he checked into the hospital more than a dozen times. He told doctors that the voices wouldn't let him sleep, that they wouldn't give him any peace. Jackson Browne hired him for his road band in 1978. Browne and Gordon jogged together and played fiercely competitive games of racquetball. "We played all the time," Browne told Rehfeld. "It was pretty well known that he'd had a breakdown, but I wanted him on the tour. You just wanted to root for him. He cut such a gallant figure, with his open white silk shirts and felt Borsalino hat, and he was such a good drummer. He'd get my attention with this great fill, really imaginative. He just rose to the occasion."

But the voices told Gordon to hang up on Bob Dylan when he called to ask him to play on *Slow Train Coming*. After that, Paul Anka offered him a job playing in a Las Vegas casino. Gordon flew out there and started to learn Anka's act, but the voice of his mother told him he had to quit. That was the end of his music career.

On June 1, 1983, Gordon called his mother and said, "You're bugging me again. I'm going to kill you." By then, she was frightened enough that she was writing down everything he said. On June 2, she called a Van Nuys city attorney attempting to get a restraining order, but she couldn't penetrate the system. The night of June 3, her son picked out a butcher knife and sharpened it. Gordon put the knife and a claw hammer in a case and drove to the Van Nuys condo of his 72-year-old mother. When she came to the door, he knocked her down with the hammer and then bashed it against her skull three more times. Afterward he stabbed her in the chest three times, leaving the knife inside her. When the police went to notify Gordon that his mother had been murdered, they found him sobbing and drunk on his living room floor.

———

LAYLA AND OTHER ASSORTED LOVE SONGS BY DEREK AND THE DOMINOS

His attorneys called the murder a tragedy and entered a plea of not guilty by reason of insanity, but California had enacted laws that greatly restricted the defense. Jim Gordon was convicted of second-degree murder, and his sentence was 16 years to life. Frightful to the judge and Gordon's parole boards were his stated lack of remorse at the time of the killing and his continuing psychosis. Rehfeld, the *Rolling Stone* writer, claimed Gordon said the voice he now heard in prison was his brother's. The voice nagged him not to eat desserts. Gordon has finished serving the minimum, but it's likely that he will never be released.

Bobby Whitlock is completely unforgiving of his long-time friend. Whitlock said of Gordon to this author, "He does not deserve *any* air time. Neither do Charles Manson or the guy that killed John Lennon. The less said about those people, the better."

There are two accounts of what happened at Gordon's penal institution when Clapton was presented with a 1992 Grammy for the inclusion of "Layla" on his *Unplugged* album, following the death of his son. Gordon, who as the credited songwriter was a co-honoree, was watching the ceremony on TV. Some say that when the award was presented, Gordon went to the bathroom and missed the segment entirely. Others say the prison block echoed with the howl of his tormented screams.

In November 2005 I received a handwritten letter from Jim Gordon. Following up on an earlier exchange, Gordon wrote that he never killed anyone, that he had been wrongfully arrested and charged with his mother's killing by the Los Angeles Police Department.

"Plus in closing," he wrote, "honest I did not break up

Derek and the Dominos. I didn't know what happened. Everyone left."

—————

For many years, Eric Clapton has been one of rock's foremost philanthropists, raising prodigious amounts of money for victims of the world's woes and pouring out songs and chords that hearten and console. Since 1998 he has dedicated much of his energy and resources to an addiction recovery center he founded on the island of Antigua. No longer the peacock he once was, he is given now to wire-rimmed glasses and stubble, and a mismatch of frumpy shorts, khakis, running shoes, and baggy shirts. Married to Melia McEnery, a young woman from Ohio whom he met at a charity auction in 1999, Clapton is a doting father to their two young daughters. He is also close to a grown daughter who was born in Montserrat—her mother was one of his lovers when his marriage to Pattie was coming apart. Clapton has become the scholar of old bluesmen who ought not be forgotten and a sage and mentor to hot young guitarists, a carefully chosen few. He has twice been honored for his contributions to music by the Queen of England.

Clapton remained a close friend of George Harrison until the former Beatle's death from cancer in 2001.

The brilliant engineer Tom Dowd, whom a mature Clapton valued as a great friend, passed away from respiratory disease in 2002.

Pattie Boyd is a photographer who lives outside London; a San Francisco show of her images from the sixties and seventies won much attention and praise in 2005. She and Eric have lunch occasionally. She's still beautiful.

—————

A magazine writer asked her to comment on what it was like to be the model and inspiration for songs such as "Something" and "Layla."

"I thought it was a great tribute and an honor," she answered. "I was very flattered."

In a *Rolling Stone* interview shortly after winning the Grammy for his unplugged version of "Layla," Clapton reminisced about Carl Radle, the *461 Ocean Boulevard* comeback, and the demise of his two backup bands. "Carl was like my brother. He brought me out of my seclusion when I was taking heroin and after the Dominos broke up. He stayed in touch . . . and said this could be our new band. And it was. And then drugs got into that, and booze, and it created a monster again. I broke up that band because we were all fucked up, we were killing one another, fighting onstage.

"And it was all drug-related. And within 6 months, Carl was dead. At that point, I was doing two bottles of brandy a day, and I couldn't lift a finger to help anybody. Now I look at it and see what a waste and what a great player he was, and I'm sad."

Clapton chose a telling metaphor in describing the band that helped him conceive *Layla*. "We peaked so quickly and made so much money. And these guys . . . were suddenly thrust into all this money and drugs and women, and it just cartwheeled, took off and blew up. It was like a massive car crash, and scary, scary, scary. We couldn't even talk to each other, we were so drugged out and paranoid. It was doomed, really. I don't think it could have been salvaged by anybody."

The *Rolling Stone* interviewer asked Clapton whether he had ever communicated with Gordon.

"I'm scared to death of that," Clapton replied. "A part of me says I owe it to him to try and get in touch. But I'm scared.

I was scared of him at the end of Derek and the Dominos. One of the reasons we broke up was the rapport between me and Jim, which had always been so good, had broken down."

So they're left with what they accomplished. Dave Marsh wrote in *The Rolling Stone Illustrated History of Rock and Roll*: "There are few moments in the repertoire of recorded rock where a singer or writer has reached so deeply into himself that the effect of hearing them is akin to witnessing a murder or suicide. . . . To me, 'Layla' is the greatest of them." In his book *Mystery Train*, Greil Marcus reflected that the journey transported Clapton to the hero who most inspired him. "All of Eric Clapton's love for Robert Johnson's music came to bear not when Clapton sang Johnson songs, but when, once Johnson's music became part of who Clapton was, Clapton came closest to himself: in the passion of 'Layla' and 'Anyday.' Finally, after years of practice and imitation, Johnson's sound was Clapton's sound: there was no way to separate the two men, nor any need to."

Nor, in that span of his life, can Clapton be separated from the collaborators who made that music with him.

For nearly 25 years, Bobby Whitlock just quit. He was always playing, learning new instruments, spending money on recording equipment for friends who might want to use it, but he thought he had to give up the life. He'd come too close to the brink. He went back to Mississippi, married, raised two children, and was an eccentric farmer. Since 1999 he has returned to his professional love and launched a second career with his new wife and partner, CoCo Carmel. For 12 years she was the wife—after Bonnie—of Delaney Bramlett.

Whitlock has been through some very hard times: a bankruptcy, an attempt by members of his family to commit him, a scary brush with the rare disease that deafened Beethoven, and, in a nightmarish episode reminiscent of the movie *Hustle and Flow,* his son, a talented hip-hop singer, was badly shot while fighting for his life and that of his pregnant wife against a gang of hooded Memphis thugs who kicked their door open to rob them. Bobby has a grandchild because of his son's bravery. He also has a daughter.

Bobby and CoCo, a statuesque blonde who sings and plays the guitar and saxophone in their performances, have been living in Nashville. One recent New Year's Eve they held an audience in thrall at the Kennedy Center in Washington. He has short hair now, and he's inked up on his chest and shoulders. He wears small ear- and nose rings and, in the style of his old blues mentors, he steps out in striking Italian suits and open-collared shirts.

One bright December day in 2005, Whitlock is on his way out of a Chinese café where we've had lunch. He spots a lonely old woman sitting by herself in a booth. He's over there at once, pouring her tea, telling her Merry Christmas, leaving her with a grateful smile on her face. Bobby sees CoCo and me staring at this act of kindness. He shoots his cuffs and says, "It's my job." Whitlock has moved on in his life and in his music, as has Clapton. But how can either of them not pause and treasure Derek and the Dominos and *Layla and Other Assorted Love Songs*? Bobby thinks often of those concerts at the Fillmore East in 1970. "We were as tight as bark," he recalls with a smile of conviction. "On our worst night, we were the best rock 'n' roll band on the planet."

VICTIMS AND SURVIVORS

SOURCES

MY INVALUABLE TOUR GUIDE was Bobby Whitlock, who first generously consented to 2 days of interviews in Nashville and in the course of those encounters and many subsequent phone calls and e-mails became my friend. Whitlock is incredibly articulate and has a pinpoint memory: In my double-checking as a reporter, no story that he told me failed to check out. I am also indebted to his mother, LaVada (Bitsy) King, for allowing her son to share with me her eloquent, not-yet-published family memoir, *When I Left Alto.* On December 31, 2003, Bobby and CoCo performed songs from *Layla* and *All Things Must Pass,* and new material in an hour-long acoustic set at the John F. Kennedy Center for Performing Arts in Washington, DC. News of the careers and future performance dates of Bobby and his wife CoCo Carmel can be found at bobbywhitlock.com.

Shortly after I began work on this book, publishers announced that Eric Clapton was writing a memoir. Representatives of Clapton discouraged me from thinking that at this time he might want to share his recollections of Derek and the Dominos with me. For someone who in recent decades has cultivated a reputation of being wary of the press, he has in fact talked a great deal about his music and personal life. Marc Roberty has enjoyed greater access to Clapton than any other journalist, and I frequently turned with confidence to three Roberty books: *Eric Clapton: In His Own Words* (Omnibus, London, 1993); *Eric Clapton: The Complete Recording Sessions 1963–1992* (St. Martin's Press, New York, 1993); and *Slowhand: The Life and Music of Eric Clapton* (Harmony Books, New York, 1991).

Of the many biographies of Clapton, for varied reasons I found these three most trustworthy: Michael Schumacher, *Crossroads: The Life and Music of Eric Clapton* (Hyperion, New York, 1995); Christopher Sandford, *Clapton: Edge of Darkness* (Da Capo, New York, 1999); and Harry Shapiro, *Eric Clapton: Lost in the Blues* (Da Capo, New York, 1992).

Many extensive interviews of Clapton are available both in print and audio. The most illuminating for me were those included in a special Clapton issue of *The Best of Guitar Player* (April, 1992), the Albert Watson interview that accompanied a *Rolling Stone* cover story, "Eric Clapton's Blues" (October 17, 1971), and a BBC interview (February 3, 1990). Probably the best telling of this story in short form is Gene Santoro's essay and liner notes for *The Layla Sessions: 20th Anniversary Edition* in 1990. A near-complete listing of the many articles about and interviews of the star is available on a dynamic Web site, www.rockbackpages.com, the online library of rock 'n' roll.

I corresponded with Jim Gordon at the prison where he resides in California, and I interviewed Carole Kaye, the legendary bass player who was his friend in the Wrecking Crew of Los Angeles studio musicians. Barry Rehfield's "When the Voices Take Over" in *Rolling Stone* (June 6, 1985) is a chilling account of the schizophrenia that led to the homicide for which he remains incarcerated. Martin Booe's "Bang the Drum Slowly" in the *Washington Post* (July 3, 1994)—written on the occasion of the unplugged "Layla" winning a Grammy—is evidently the last time Gordon consented to an interview. Gordon was a great musician and an essential member of Derek and the Dominos; I wish the co-author of "Layla" well.

A close woman friend of Carl Radle who wished to remain anonymous provided much insight into the affable bass player and longtime Clapton sideman and confidant. Bobby Whitlock was my lead source on the rollicking days at Leon Russell's Plantation, where Whitlock befriended Radle. A commemorative Web site, carlradle.com, provides biographical data and a collection of his fine photography. My friends Jimmy LaFave and Kip Stratton, both of whom spent their formative years in Oklahoma, kindled my interest in the fascinating Tulsa rock scene that produced Radle, Russell, Jim Keltner, J. J. Cale, and many other stellar musicians. A lively and entertaining Web Site, tulsa_time_w.htm, provides a never-ending store of Tulsa musical knowledge and memories.

Duane Allman died just as he was becoming a public figure. Along with the impressions he made on Clapton and Whitlock, the Dominos' fifth member left behind an incisive interview by Ellen Mandel in *Guitar World* (November 1981), and Allman's teenage friend and rock 'n' roll mentor, Jim Shepley, contributed an insightful and vivid essay, "How to Play Slide," to a package of articles about Allman in

Guitar Player (November 1992). Scott Freeman's *Midnight Riders: The Story of the Allman Brothers Band* (Little, Brown; Boston, 1995) rankles some fans and band members in its emphases and conclusions, but from Freeman's days in the early 1980s as a reporter for the *Macon Telegraph and News,* his research of the band has been solid and his book remains to this date the best-documented study of Allman's short life and career. *Rhythm and the Blues: A Life in American Music,* by storied record producer Jerry Wexler and David Ritz (Knopf, New York, 1993), offers expert perspective on the talent and personality of one of Wexler's favorite guitarists. Peter Guralnick's *Sweet Soul Music: Rhythm and Blues and the Southern Dream of Freedom* (Harper & Row, New York, 1986) ably details the Memphis and Muscle Shoals music scenes that propelled the careers of both Allman and Bobby Whitlock. Cameron Crowe's December 6, 1973, *Rolling Stone* cover spread "The Allman Brothers Story"—written when the journalist and screenwriter was a teenager—focuses on Gregg Allman but richly illuminates the growth of his band and his relationship with Duane. Randy Poe's *Skydog: The Duane Allman Story* (Backbeat Books, San Francisco, 2006) will doubtless add much to the story.

As this book was nearing completion, a San Francisco keyboard player and critic, J. D. Smith, tracked me down and shared many insights and firsthand memories of events that would have eluded me. Smith's review of one of the Derek and the Dominos' Fillmore East concerts in October 1971 was published on a Web site of Clapton's 1975 album *E. C. Was Here.*

Bob Spitz's *The Beatles: The Biography* (Little, Brown; New York, 2005) is an authoritative and well-written source for everything one wishes to know about the English quartet—it pays much attention to the marriage of George Harrison and Pattie Boyd and their friendship with Clapton. The woman who inspired "Something" and "Layla" has since been interviewed and profiled by the British magazine *Hello!* (July 11, 1992), the London *Daily Telegraph* (March 17, 1999), and, on the occasion of the December 2004 exhibit in San Francisco of her photography, by CNN.

Mark Moorman's much-praised 2004 documentary *Tom Dowd and the Language of Music* ably tells the story of the pioneering engineer and producer and demonstrates, using the original master tapes, how he mixed the lead guitars of Clapton and Allman on *Layla*. Also useful is Derek Halsey's October 27, 2002, profile and tribute in the online magazine *Gritz*. Another good source is an interview of Dowd in *Tone Quest Report,* a discussion reprinted by http://network.real-media.com.

The Arabic legend and love story of Layla and Majnun and the Persian epic poem of Nizami Ganjavi have been studied, interpreted, written about, and translated throughout the world. Especially illuminating for this author was a 1998 essay, "The Man Who Loved Too Much," by Jean-Pierre Guinhut, a French scholar and career diplomat who was then France's ambassador to Azerbaijan. The essay was published in *Azerbaijani International.* The story of the legend and book is further told in the British Library's Online Gallery of Asian and African Manuscripts.

Sections on the American blues singers and guitarists cited by Eric Clapton as inspirations in interviews I've mentioned were drawn from a large number of books, articles, and Web sites on American rhythm and blues. In addition to

Gene Santoro's essay for the rerelease of *Layla and Other Assorted Love Songs*, I also found instructive liner notes for other albums, some short and some long: Eric Clapton for his albums *Me and Mr. Johnson* and *Reptile*; Tony Glover for *Duane Allman: An Anthology;* J. P. Bean for Joe Cocker's *Mad Dogs and Englishmen;* and Rob Bowman for the Band's *Music from Big Pink.*

Finally, in writing about this and other popular American and British music, I began with Dave Marsh's critique of Clapton in *The Rolling Stone Illustrated History of Rock and Roll* (Random House, New York, third edition, 1992), Greil Marcus's frequently revised and updated *Mystery Train: Images of America in Rock 'n' Roll Music* (Penguin, New York, 1977), and Bill C. Malone, *Country Music U.S.A.* (University of Texas, Austin, 1968).

SELECTED DISCOGRAPHY

Duane Allman, *An Anthology*, volumes I and II. (Polydor 1972, 1974)

The Allman Brothers Band, *At Fillmore East (Remastered)* (Mercury/Universal, 1997)

The Band, *Music from Big Pink* (Capitol, 2000)

Eric Clapton, *Crossroads* (Polydor, 1988)

Eric Clapton, *Eric Clapton* (Polydor, 1970)

Eric Clapton, *Me and Mr. Johnson* (Reprise/Wea, 2004)

Joe Cocker, *Mad Dogs and Englishmen* (A&M, 1999)

Delaney and Bonnie and Friends, *On Tour with Eric Clapton* (Atlantic, 1970)

Derek and the Dominos, *Layla and Other Assorted Love Songs (Remixed Version): Twentieth Anniversary Edition* (Polydor, 1990)

Derek and the Dominos, *Live at the Fillmore* (Polydor, 1994)

George Harrison, *All Things Must Pass (Remastered Edition),* (Capitol, 2001)

Bobby Whitlock, *Bobby Whitlock* (ABC Dunhill, 1972)

Bobby Whitlock, *Raw Velvet* (ABC Dunhill, 1972)

Bobby Whitlock and Kim Carmel, *Other Assorted Love Songs* (Domino Records, 2003)